THE WORLD OF THE MOOSE

LIVING WORLD BOOKS

John K. Terres, Editor

The World of the American Elk by Joe Van Wormer
The World of the Ant by David F. Costello
The World of the Beaver by Leonard Lee Rue III
The World of the Bison by Ed Park
The World of the Black Bear by Joe Van Wormer
The World of the Bobcat by Joe Van Wormer
The World of the Bottlenosed Dolphin
     by David K. and Melba C. Caldwell
The World of the Canada Goose by Joe Van Wormer
The World of the Coyote by Joe Van Wormer
The World of the Frog and the Toad by George Porter
The World of the Great Horned Owl
     by G. Ronald Austing and John B. Holt, Jr.
The World of the Grizzly Bear by W. J. Schoonmaker
The World of the Gull by David F. Costello
The World of the Moose by Joe Van Wormer
The World of the Opossum by James F. Keefe
The World of the Otter by Ed Park
The World of the Porcupine by David F. Costello
The World of the Prairie Dog by David F. Costello
The World of the Pronghorn by Joe Van Wormer
The World of the Raccoon by Leonard Lee Rue III
The World of the Red Fox by Leonard Lee Rue III
The World of the Red-tailed Hawk by G. Ronald Austing
The World of the Snake by Hal H. Harrison
The World of the Swan by Joe Van Wormer
The World of the White-tailed Deer by Leonard Lee Rue III
The World of the Wolf
     by Russell J. Rutter and Douglas H. Pimlott
The World of the Woodchuck by W. J. Schoonmaker

The World of the Moose

Text and Photographs by
Joe Van Wormer

J. B. Lippincott Company

Philadelphia and New York

U.S. Library of Congress Cataloging in Publication Data

Van Wormer, Joe.
   The world of the moose.

   (Living world books)
   Bibliography: p.
   1. Moose. I. Title.
QL737.U55V32   599′.7357   79–38995
ISBN–0–397–00846–5
ISBN–0–397–00868–6 (lib. bdg.)

To My Wife, Helen

Contents

THE WORLD OF THE MOOSE

A full-grown bull moose is imposing.

Meet the Moose

IT IS HIGHLY UNLIKELY that the moose will ever win a prize for good looks. Compared to the graceful white-tailed deer or the ruggedly handsome elk, it cannot, even by the most charitable, be called beautiful. It can, however, lay claim, to being the world's largest living deer and probably the largest antlered mammal that ever lived. Females, despite their homeliness, have a solemn dignity about them, and males with their massive antlers are truly impressive.

The American moose is the same species as the Old World elk, or "elg," but the early explorers of this country did not bring this name with them—at least, not for the moose. It was applied, instead, to another New World deer, the American elk, which could more accurately be called a "wapiti." * The name "moose" is derived from the Algonquian Indian language and means "he eats off" or "twig eater." This aptly describes the eating habits of the moose, and even though the name may be unfortunate because it does not agree with that of the moose's prior-named European cousins, it somehow seems to fit. Variations of the Indian name are "mons" and "mose."

* *Editor's Note:* Mr. Van Wormer has clearly explained the confusion of the terms "elk and "wapiti" in his Living World book *The World of the American Elk.*

The word "moose" is an Indian word meaning "twig eater."

The moose is an even-toed hoofed mammal in the order Artiodactyla, the family Cervidae,* the genus *Alces,* and the species *Alces alces.* There are seven living subspecies of moose in the world: one in Europe, two in Asia, and four in North America. They stem from the common ancestors of all deer, which apparently appeared in the Oligocene, some 45 million years ago, as small cat-sized animals. Antlers apparently evolved during the next 10 million years, and then somewhere in the 35 million years that followed, the species we know as moose were formed.

* *Editor's Note:* The family Cervidae—deer and allies—in North America includes the elk, or wapiti, the white-tailed and the mule deer, the moose, and the caribou or reindeer.

During the Pleistocene, or Great Ice Age (which began about 1½ million years ago), a substantial part of the North American continent was covered by ice. So much of the planet's water supply was involved that the level of the oceans was lowered to expose a land bridge, sometimes 1,000 miles wide, between North America and Asia. Until about 12,000 years ago, that land remained above water most of the time, and there was considerable animal traffic between the two continents. Despite the fact that great ice sheets covered much of North America during this period, apparently most of Alaska was completely free of ice. This gave the migrants, including the ancestors of our present-day moose, a foothold. Later, as the ice sheets receded, the animals spread to other areas. Environmental differences produced the four different subspecies now recognized in this country.

A full-grown moose measures 8 to 10 feet long from nose to tail and stands between 5½ and 7½ feet high at the shoulders. Mature cows weigh 600 to 800 pounds; mature bulls, 900 to 1,400 pounds. Alaskan and Yukon Territory bulls may reach 1,800 pounds (Palmer, 1954). Their heavy antlers have a 60- to 70-inch spread and tower 8 to 10 feet above the ground.

At a distance the moose is an ungainly black animal with light-colored legs. At close range the black, or brownish-black, is mostly on the breast, shoulders, and flanks, shading into rusty brown on the withers, back, neck, and head. The belly is lighter and the insides of the ears are whitish. From the knees down, the legs are a pale, warm gray. This coloration tends to make the animal conspicuous when it is out in the open but serves as a most effective camouflage in shadowy forests.

The appearance of the moose is so unique that it can hardly be mistaken for any other animal. It does not seem to belong to this day and age at all; it would fit more appropriately into some earlier period when hairy mammoths and similar beasts roamed the earth. Its large body is perched on long, stiltlike legs; its hindquarters are slim and

The moose is a large black animal with light-colored legs.

set lower than the massive humped forequarters. Its tail—2 or 3 inches long—is little more than an excuse and cannot even be seen a few yards away. Its short, heavy neck with a mane of long dark hair supports a long, narrow head, which is topped by a pair of large and independently mobile ears. A mature male has huge palmate antlers with small prongs projecting from the borders. The antlers of the Alaskan-Yukon moose—largest of the American forms—are often great basinlike multi-fingered scoops.

The moose has a long, narrow head, small eyes, and great basinlike antlers.

Its eyes are smallish, but the nose is large and pendulous. Its upper lip is extremely flexible and muscular.

Dangling pendantlike from the moose's throat is a dewlap of skin and hair called a "bell." Both males and females, even as calves, have them, but no one has yet determined their purpose. The bell varies in size and shape—sometimes flat, sometimes round. It may hang from the jaw or from a long bladelike dewlap running lengthwise on the neck. Ordinarily, the bell is 8 to 10 inches long, but one 38 inches

17

The nose and upper lip overhang the lower lip.

long was reported on a cow moose. As the animals grow older the length of the bell tends to decrease.

A mature moose has thirty-two teeth (Burt and Grossenheider, 1952): twelve in the upper jaw and twenty in the lower jaw. There are no incisors or canine teeth in the upper jaw, but each side has three premolars and three molars. The lower jaw has the same number of molars and premolars and, in addition, three incisors and one canine tooth on each side.

At birth the milk incisors are functional and the milk premolars are beginning to erupt. At about six months the first molars become functional, as do some of the permanent incisors at about fourteen months. At nineteen months or so the moose usually has its permanent teeth.

Moose have two pairs of external glands. The lachrymal, or tear, gland is forward and slightly below the eye. Its mildly antiseptic secretions keep the cornea moist. Metatarsal and interdigital glands are absent; the tarsal glands inside the hind legs are small.

Other than the bell, the moose's unusual features are useful and enable the animal to live in rough country. Its long, slim legs permit it to reach high for food and to travel swiftly through tangles of fallen trees. Its cloven hoofs spread widely to support its travels through marsh and muskeg.

All members of the deer family, including the moose, are unguligrade, which means they walk on the tips of their third and fourth

The moose walks on the tip of its two middle toes. The dew claws, higher up on the foot, seldom make an imprint.

toes. It is believed that they started out with five toes but that evolutionary transformation produced the present structure, which is more efficient for walking and running. One toe has disappeared completely. The remaining four include toes two and five, which form "dew claws," the horny projections on the back of the leg above the hoofs. These dew claws give the moose added footing in bogs, soft mud, and snow.

The front hoofs are larger than the back ones; those of the bull are longer than those of the cow and more blunt in front. But there is so much variation in hoof shape that determination of sex by hoof prints alone would be uncertain. Although moose tracks are generally larger and more pointed than those of elk, the difference is not always obvious, especially if the moose are young.

The tracks of adult moose measure approximately 6 inches in length and 4½ inches in width. Including dew-claw marks, they may reach 10 inches in length. However, considerable variation is reported. An Alaskan cow, for instance, had a track 5½ inches long and 5 inches wide.

The moose's senses of hearing and smell are highly developed, but its vision is not very good. It seems to be able to detect movements readily; but for identification and warnings it relies first upon its hearing, then upon its sense of smell for final confirmation.

An adult's first reaction to alarm is to turn its head toward the source, its ears cocked forward in characteristic alert posture. After a few seconds the animal may decide on flight. Disturbed cows often display their agitation by squeezing their hind legs together and urinating on their hocks.

When fleeing, moose almost always stop and look back. After entering protective cover, or having run some distance, they will pause and stand quietly, their attention directed toward their back trail.

Meet the Moose

If alerted by a glimpse of movement, such as that of a person in motion, a moose may circle downward so that its sensitive nose has a better chance to identify the movement as either potentially harmless or dangerous. Captive moose have reportedly been able to detect the footsteps of approaching persons one and one half to three minutes before the human ear became aware of the sound. Certain noises seem to elicit more response from moose than others—the snapping of twigs or high-pitched metallic noises get their attention quickly.

A moose's first reaction to potential danger is to turn its head and cock its ears forward alertly.

While feeding in shallow water, a moose often submerges its head up to the ears, which continue to move about as the animal checks for danger in different directions. If it hears a suspicious sound, it jerks its head out of the water and immediately turns its full attention toward it. The ears are raised to the alert position and focused on the noise. What the animal sees and, more important, smells will dictate its actions. These, in turn, will depend upon its past experience. Moose in protected places such as our national parks will not take flight so readily as those in areas where they are hunted.

Moose can move with unbelievable quietness through heavy cover, but they don't always do so. They may crash noisily into the brush, breaking dry branches with apparently no concern but that of getting away as quickly as possible. On hard ground their pounding hoofs are clearly audible several hundred yards away.

Some fifteen years ago I accompanied a moose-hunting expedition into Alaska in order to photograph the action. We were in the Rainy Pass section of south-central Alaska, and on the second day our guide located a trophy-size bull that was within stalking range. We spent most of the day working our way carefully upwind toward the animal. We stopped at frequent intervals to check the activity of the bull through a powerful spotting scope. At no time did he give any indication that he had noticed us. As we came within good rifle range he disappeared into a brush-choked draw. The guide sent his assistant on a wide, circling course upwind from the moose so that his scent would drift down into the draw. It took only a whiff of the man-scent to bring the bull out into the open as he moved away at a fast trot.

To obtain some of the cow and calf pictures included in this book, Jim Straley, biologist for the Wyoming Game Commission, and I combed the high country in western Wyoming around the headwaters of Green River in early June of 1969. We finally spotted a cow with a new calf, but she saw us about the same time and took off in a fast ground-covering trot with the calf following. This, Straley said, was

A cow and her calf pause uncertainly, trying to decide whether or not the intruders are dangerous.

somewhat unusual since the calf was only a few days old, at most a week. With a couple of short rest stops, the pair covered almost a mile before the cow decided to stop. It was open country, with scattered islands of aspen and other cover, so we were able to follow their progress until they halted in the fringe of an aspen grove about a half-mile long and 200 yards deep.

Reasoning that the calf would be too tired to go farther, we back-tracked and drove a long roundabout route to get on the other, down-wind, side of the aspen grove in which they were resting.

We made the last mile of the stalk into the wind on foot. Everything was just right except that we misjudged the exact location of the cow and calf by 25 yards. This was unfortunate. When we walked around a large boulder we came practically on top of them: they were no more than 50 feet away. We had arrived without our scent giving us away, but we had also hoped to get there unobserved so that I could photograph the two animals together without disturbing them.

The cow stood up and looked at us. We remained motionless, and since she couldn't get our scent she was probably uncertain about us. We were so close, however, that she soon decided we were dangerous and moved off, with the tired little calf staggering along at her heels. She stopped 50 yards away and checked us again. Her original judgment confirmed, she and the calf trotted off and disappeared into the next grove of aspen, 200 yards away.

A person watching moose in national parks or game refuges might think that the animals are paying no attention to him. Quite the reverse is true. Even though a moose may appear to be oblivious to anyone's presence, the fact is that it is pretty much aware at all times of what is going on around it. I can cite a graphic example of this.

One fall in Yellowstone National Park, two moose that I took to be yearling siblings were feeding in a marshy spot at the north end of Willow Park. They were 30 to 50 yards off the road and, I thought, unconcerned about the presence of the visitors stopping to watch and

24

photograph them. I took a number of pictures from various angles and then decided to look for a different viewpoint. I walked around one end of the marshy area and climbed up toward them along a steep slope. I hadn't gone more than a few yards before both moose trotted off and disappeared in the timber. They were obviously alert to everything I was doing, and when it looked as if I was going to cut off their line of retreat, they became frightened and left.

A moose's reaction to danger signals is sometimes bewildering. At first they may show no alarm and remain quietly facing the disturbance. Then, after a short interval, they may move slowly away and, finally, break into a trot toward the safety of protective cover.

While hiking along a sagebrush-covered bench overlooking the Snake River, I came upon a cow moose feeding in a small pond in the river bottom below me. She looked up, motionless for thirty seconds, while water dripped noisily from her head, and then slowly waded to shore. A calf I had not noticed got up and greeted her. The cow briefly nibbled at some willows: then the two walked to a shallow arm of the river and waded across. Once on the other side and a hundred yards away, the cow broke into a trot. The calf followed suit, and they disappeared into the brush.

Moose, being large animals, seem to require a comparatively large minimum area per animal. Also, they are less social than other deer and show little inclination to form definite herds. Closest association is between a cow and her calf or, occasionally, her yearlings. A bull and a cow, along with her calf if she has one, stay together for a while during the rutting season. Yearling siblings may also travel together for a time.

Other than on these occasions, moose in close proximity are influenced only casually, if at all, by one another. Generally, such gatherings, if they can be called that, result from a concentration of available

A cow moose stopped feeding when I appeared, and soon led her youngster across the river. They lost no time seeking the protection of the brush.

food. There is no leadership or social hierarchy demonstrated, and the animals move about independently of one another. There does not appear to be resentment among the members of these loosely associated groups; nor do they seem to seek one another's company. Yet groups sometimes persist for rather lengthy periods.

Although these three bulls seem to be "together," it is probable that only the abundance of food brought each to the meadow.

In July, 1969, I made a trip into the Grand Teton National Park–Yellowstone National Park area to photograph bull moose with well-developed antlers that were still in the velvet. Douglas B. Houston, biologist with the Grand Teton National Park, told me of a group of four to five bull moose that came out each afternoon to feed in the meadows below Lewis River Falls in Yellowstone National Park. This falls is 100 yards or so west of the south entrance road, about 10 miles inside the park. For about a mile the road parallels the Lewis River and the meadows, which are several hundred yards wide in places.

When I arrived, around 4 P.M., three bulls were grazing along the river bank no more than 20 yards from the busy highway. A fourth was striding purposefully across the meadow toward them. They were fat and sleek in their short summer coats; their great antlers were about two-thirds grown. They fed industriously, paying little attention to one another or to the gathering crowd of interested park visitors who were obviously thrilled at seeing the four great beasts at close range. As often happens, some of the watchers got too close, and the disturbed moose moved across the Lewis River to feed on low-lying browse on the other side.

The four continued to graze for about an hour, moving 100 yards or so up the meadow in the process. Two fed a few feet apart for fifteen or twenty minutes with complete disregard for each other. After about a half-hour a fifth bull came out of the timber and started feeding 200 yards away. A little later one of the bulls lay down, and in a few minutes two others "joined" him. The fourth one also lay down but on the opposite side of the stream, between 50 and 75 yards away. The first three were within 30 feet of one another.

There seemed to be some relationship here, although what it was and how strong it was would be pure guesswork. However, the fact that they had been seen together with considerable regularity for an extended period indicated that the continuing association was not

Moose are basically solitary creatures.

entirely accidental. Possibly, the explanation is simply that there was an abundance of food in the meadow.

Loosely associated groups of up to six moose which acted in much the same way as these Lewis River bulls were reported in an Alaskan study. No leader or dominant animal was recognizable among these Alaskan animals, but generally when one moose left an open meadow and disappeared in the brush, the others would follow one at a time by the same route within five or ten minutes. Sometimes a member of the group that had not finished feeding would continue grazing for another half-hour or so. When it did leave, however, it followed approximately the same path as the others.

Agonistic behavior * between females seems to be common throughout the year, and females with calves are aggressive toward all other

* *Editor's Note:* Term of animal behaviorists (ethologists) for attacking, fleeing, threatening, and submissive behavior of animals.

moose during winter periods. Both adult males and adult females show aggressive behavior toward yearling males during spring and summer; however, such behavior is not often seen among adult males. Aggression may take the form of actual or attempted physical contact or be merely "head high" or "head low" threat postures.

Agonistic behavior influences the summer travels of yearlings and tends to move them into places that have low adult populations. This appears to maintain the moose's quasi-solitary social organization and cause the spread of moose populations.

Moose also show little inclination for vocal communication except during the rutting season. Other than that they mostly remain silent,* although there are some vocal exchanges between cows and their calves. Tagging teams have reported that calves give a low-toned grunt when metal tags are placed in their ears. High-pitched grunts or bleat-ings that have also been noted appear to be distress signals. Cows may reply to this call with several low-pitched grunts. Grunts from a cow also seem to serve to call a calf to her.

Adults of both sexes produce an alarm call which has been variously described as a "bark"—a hoarse sound somewhat between the barking of a dog and the mooing of a cow—and not unlike that caused by the rapid drawing of a wood rasp across a loosely held piece of plywood.

Although moose live in the coniferous forest areas of the north, they do not, as might be thought, favor the dense mature growth. Their preference is for open places where logging or fire has destroyed the old trees and secondary growths have produced an abundance of moose food. They like the openings where willow, aspen, and birch surround marshes or bodies of water containing aquatic plants to

* *Editor's Note:* According to de Vos (1958), the moose in Ontario, Canada, call throughout the year and utter three distinct calls: an alarm call used by both sexes, a whine used by the calves and yearlings to attract the mother, and a short grunt used by females to attract their young.

31

Moose like open places for foraging, especially with water nearby containing aquatic plants to supplement their diet.

supplement their bark and twig browse diets. They do use the dense conifer growth for resting and escape cover.

Good moose habitat does not necessarily remain good. The essential ingredient is forest succession or regeneration. Moose populations rise during the early stages of forest succession and decline as the forest matures. A combination of climax trees, second-growth shrubs, and saplings with young growth predominating provides the best habitat and supplies a variety of preferred foods.

Thickets and heavier growth are good for resting and escape cover.

Moose tend to stay in one locality as long as the food supply is ample. If not forced to move because of browse shortages, a cow may spend her entire life within 10 miles of her birthplace. Bulls may wander a bit more during the rutting period. In the Jackson Hole–Grand Teton area, both winter and summer ranges were usually less than 1½ square miles in area.

The former range of the moose shown in the map on page 34 is reprinted from *The Mammals of North America* by E. Raymond Hall

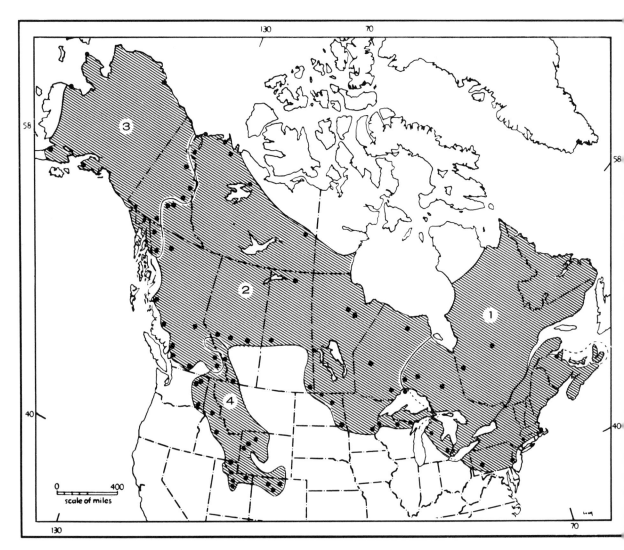

Former Range of the Moose
(Alces Alces)

1. A. a. americana   2. A. a. andersoni   3. A. a. gigs   4. A. a. shirasi

(From The Mammals of North America, copyright © 1959 The Ronald Press Company, New York. Reprinted by permission of the publisher.)

and Keith R. Kelson. In his book *North American Moose*, Randolph L. Peterson gives substantially the same areas for the moose's present range, although he indicates that some shrinkage has occurred, especially in the southern parts.

Peterson depicts the northern limit of moose distribution to be a line that extends from Anticosti Island, off the east coast of Canada, to central James Bay; it slopes northwesterly to Great Bear Lake in the Northwest Territories. South of the Canadian border, the animal has been eliminated from its former range in New York, New Jersey, Pennsylvania, Connecticut, Rhode Island, Massachusetts, Ohio, and South Dakota.

There are now only remnant populations in Michigan, New Hampshire, North Dakota, Utah, Vermont, Washington, and Wisconsin. An occasional moose is seen in northwestern Colorado, but no population has ever been established there and these are considered to be migrants from Wyoming.

Today, significant numbers of moose are in Maine, northeastern Minnesota, western Montana, northern Idaho, western Wyoming, most of Alaska except in the extreme west and north, and all across the wooded regions of Canada. This includes parts of all the provinces and territories. However, in Canada they are not along the Pacific Coast west of the mountains nor on the islands off the Alaskan and Canadian Pacific Coast. On the Atlantic Ocean side of Canada, both Nova Scotia and Newfoundland have moose. The Newfoundland population is the result of a highly successful introduction in 1904.

In some areas, moose have extended their range in the last fifty years. Wyoming has reported population gains, and in the central interior of British Columbia only a few moose could be found until after 1900. Indians of the Cariboo, Chilcotin, and other parts of the interior had no word for moose in their native languages. The animal was new to them. The reason for its southward migration was the cutting and burning of the dense forests by settlers and miners. Huge

The Alaskan tundra—an example of the wild and remote habitat the moose prefers.

areas were opened up, and when food suitable for moose appeared, so did the moose.

A similar situation seems to have developed on the Kenai Peninsula of Alaska, which contained few, if any, moose before the great forest

fire of 1883. Since then, moose have moved into the area and have become abundant. The 1,730,000-acre Kenai National Moose Range, a wildlife refuge established primarily to protect moose, is on this peninsula.

It is impossible to obtain an accurate census of moose and of many wide-ranging wildlife species. As a matter of fact, it is often impossible to get even an educated guess, since game management personnel in particular are reluctant to make population estimates. They prefer to report simply whether the species is increasing or decreasing. This they can do with some degree of accuracy from obtainable data.

Nevertheless, population estimates are occasionally made—and it is as hard to prove them wrong as to prove them right. In what he called a "rough estimate," Ernest Thompson Seton calculated over a half-century ago that there was a primitive population of a million moose in North America. He determined that the entire moose range was about 3,500,000 square miles, but, as the range was not all equally good, it would take about 3½ square miles to sustain one moose. Randolph L. Peterson suggested that "in eastern North America an average density of 1 moose per 5 square miles might be regarded as normal."

In the Big Game Inventory for 1968, Wildlife Leaflet 487, published by the Fish and Wildlife Service, United States Department of the Interior, population figures for moose compiled from information provided by the various states were:

Alaska	140,000
Maine	13,000
Michigan	25
Minnesota	7,000
New Hampshire	200
North Dakota	20
Vermont	25
Washington	50
Wisconsin	25
Wyoming	3,500
TOTAL	163,845

States with moose population estimates that were obtained from various other sources:

Idaho		2,000
Montana		3,600
Utah		100
	TOTAL	5,700
TOTAL U.S. POPULATION		169,545

Because of the wild and remote nature of much of the country involved, there is little chance of obtaining even a fair approximation of Canada's moose population. If Canada has as many moose as the United States, the North American population would be about 350,000. If Canada has twice as many, which is possible, the total estimated population would be approximately a half-million.

In the spring, moose shed their ragged winter coats.

Spring

SPRING COMES LATE in moose country, and the drifted snow melts slowly. The first patches of green grass to appear are eagerly sought by moose tired of a winter-long diet of twigs and limbs. It has been reported that they kneel and graze on the grass in that position for as long as two hours at a time. In late March and early April they paw through the snow to feed on lichens, ground birch, or green shoots of grass.

As the moose adapts to the changing seasons it begins to shed its worn and ragged winter coat. During the long, cold months the hair has faded and bleached to a light gray-brown. Adult males are the first to shed. The process starts around the shoulder hump, progresses along the back of the neck, down the front legs, and along the back to the rump. Shedding may be complete as early as June 1, but moose with some patches of winter hair have been noted as late as July 2. During the molt they present a scraggly appearance, and large bunches of shed hair can be found at salt licks and along the trails.

After shedding, the moose's new coat is thin and short, and almost black in the older bulls. Younger bulls, cows, and yearlings are a rich cocoa brown.

In the southern parts of moose territory, movements onto spring

41

ranges begin in late March. Generally, the moose is nonmigratory, at least in comparison with, say, the caribou. However, some moose in the mountain regions of the West make seasonal movements—from winter ranges in the river valleys to spring and summer ranges on the higher slopes.

Tagged moose in Jackson Hole have traveled up to 20 miles between summer and winter ranges. Most movements on and off seasonal ranges are due to changes in snow depths. This is not a hard and fast rule however. Some moose—notably cows, calves, and yearlings—remain in the lower, or winter, ranges the entire year. Palatability and availability of food, more than anything else, seem to govern seasonal movements. In one Montana study area, moose were in or near the lower meadows in late spring, moved into high country during the summer, and then went down to lower country again in September. A month later they were back on the timbered slopes for two months and then returned to the lowlands for the winter. Later, when the willows were all eaten and the snows too deep for feeding, they were back on the ridges.

Not all moose retreat before winter's snows. Some have been seen in the Grand Teton National Park at altitudes of 9,000 feet in snow 5 to 6 feet deep. In midwinter, moose in Yellowstone National Park have been observed on the high ridges, where they feed on the twigs and branches of lodgepole pine, fir, and whatever deciduous shrubs are available. On Michigan's Isle Royale, moose are sometimes seen on the ridges, where the snow is not so deep as it is in lower country where there is better food.

The antlers of a mature moose are truly magnificent structures of pure bone that are shed and regrown each year. Normally, only the males are so equipped, but occasional females with antlers have been seen. Such antlers are usually poorly developed and are the result of a glandular abnormality.

Antler growth begins early in April but is not noticeable until the

Moose look sleek and trim in their new coats.

Antler growth starts as mere "velvet" knobs.
By mid-July antlers are about two-thirds developed.

latter half of the month. Development is from two projections of the frontal bone known as pedicels, which are midway between the eyes and the ears. The antlers grow outward almost at right angles to the head and then sweep upward.

Antlers first appear as mere swellings but soon develop into velvet-covered knobs. This so-called velvet is soft skin covered with fine hair which covers the flexible bony material of the growing antlers and carries a network of blood vessels that provides nourishment for them. During May and June the antlers progress rapidly and by mid-July are about two-thirds grown.

During the early stages antlers are easily damaged, and such injuries can cause deformities. If the pedicel is damaged, the deformity recurs with each new set of antlers.

A few years ago some friends of mine were hunting moose with famous Alaskan guide Bud Branham. After several days, during which only small bulls were seen, Branham located a bull a mile away that appeared through the powerful spotting scope to have unusually large antlers. He and his hunter made a careful stalk that lasted several hours. Finally within range, they eased into position, with the animal standing broadside a hundred yards distant, unaware of their presence. He was dispatched with one well-placed shot.

From where they stood, the antlers looked monstrous, but when they reached the fallen monarch they saw that one antler—unfortunately the one on the side away from them which they had not been able to see—was deformed, apparently as the result of an injury during the early stages of its growth. The normal antler was very large, and after measuring its spread from the tip to the center of the animal's forehead, they doubled it to see what the spread might have been had the deformed antler been healthy. They were extremely disappointed to discover that, had both antlers been normal, the animal would have had a greater spread than any then on record.

When antler development is complete, ossification begins at the base

Remnants of velvet stick to the antlers. The points remain white and polished.

and progresses upward until the entire antler becomes rigid and hard. At this time—the middle of August or later—the velvet starts to dry and strip off, a process the moose helps along by rubbing his antlers against trees and bushes.

46

Some blood remains in the drying velvet, and stains may appear. The uncovered antlers are almost white at first, but continual rubbing against trees and brush stains them and produces a polished tan, which gradually changes to a dark brown. The points remain white and polished, however.

I have seen mature bulls in late September that still had some dried remnants of old velvet stuck to the concave surfaces of the palmated part of the antler. This was probably because those parts of the antler are not reached when the animal rubs them against brush.

Antler growth is accomplished in a period of about four months and is a truly remarkable phenomenon. The antlers of a mature Alaskan bull moose, for example, weigh from 60 to 85 pounds. According to Hamilton (1939), antlers are the most rapid-growing membrane bones of mammals.

The principal function of antlers appears to be related to sexual selection; they are used mainly in fights between rival males for desirable females (Carrington, 1963). During the fall, when the antlers are in prime condition, they may also be used against other animals, but normally the sharp hoofs of both male and female are their primary weapons.

Antler shedding generally begins during the last half of December but has been reported as early as November 29. Healthy mature bulls shed first, and shedding is generally over by early January. Younger bulls shed later—two-year-olds in April, for example—but they drop their antlers earlier each year until they reach maturity.

The bull calf may develop horn "buttons" with caps on them that are visible above the hair. During the latter part of his first winter these are rubbed off. At sixteen months of age the young bull wears his first antlers. They are 6 to 10 inches long and may be spiked, forked, or flattened. The size and shape show considerable variation among individuals. The following year the antlers are longer and develop prongs on either side. The third set of antlers, which mature

The best antlers come from bulls between six and ten years old.

These antlers come from a bull past his prime.

when the moose is about forty months old, show some palmation. The four-year-old male displays the typical adult antler form, but it is small. Antlers continue to develop and grow larger each year until the animal reaches his prime, at around seven years of age. The best-developed antlers come from bulls between the ages of six and ten. After that, antler growth tends to retrogress. The antlers of males past their prime may weigh less but have a beam larger than that of younger animals. They are also apt to be less symmetrical.

Very old moose develop antlers with few points and little palmation, and these have been compared to the horns of long-horned cattle.

In the Boone and Crockett Club's compilation of big-game records the greatest antler spread for the Alaskan moose (*Alces alces gigas*) is 77½ inches. The widest spread for the Wyoming moose (*Alces alces shirasi*) is 53 inches, and for the Canadian moose (for which the club lists both *Alces alces americana* and *Alces alces andersoni*) the greatest spread is 71⅝ inches.

Development of antlers this size requires optimum conditions: adequate food supply, high mineral content of soil, and inherited characteristics. Weather may also be a factor.

49

These massive antlers may not seem at all compatible with the dense forest areas through which bulls frequently travel, but the animals apparently have great depth perception and can judge accurately the spaces they can pass through without striking their antlers against the trees. In narrow spaces, they turn their heads sideways.

Despite the obvious fact that antlers vary with age, their characteristics provide a poor basis for determining the age of mature moose. About all that can be said is that an animal is either mature or past maturity, but this has its drawbacks because a mature animal in poor health might appear older than an old one in excellent health. During the animal's first three years of life, antler growth bears some relation to age, but the variations in development are so great as to sometimes restrict the classifying of all such to an under-four-year-old group.*

A calf stays with its mother all through its first winter and far into spring. It has been protected and fed and has learned to feed itself under the tutelage of a formidable guardian. It has had little if any contact with other moose except for a sibling, if it has one, and a bull that may have been attentive to the cow for a brief period during the mating season. About two weeks before the next calf is due, usually in early May, the heavily pregnant cow turns on the calf and drives it away by running at it, making other threatening gestures, or actually striking it with her front hoofs.

This treatment thoroughly confuses the calf. Its whole world has suddenly gone awry. Its first reaction seems to be one of complete disbelief, and it tries again and again to rejoin the cow. After a dozen

---

* *Editor's Note:* The structure of teeth, their development and wear, has been the basis for determining the ages of some mammals. C. W. Severinghaus (1949) developed a technique for determining the ages of white-tailed deer (see *The World of the White-tailed Deer,* by Leonard Lee Rue III, a Living World book), and Peterson (1955) used a similar method to determine the ages of moose.

or two rejections the yearling learns to keep at a safe distance, usually a 100 yards or so. In this manner it can, to a degree, stay with its mother and follow her general movements and activities. Its big problem is that it must now make decisions for itself: when and where to feed, when and where to rest and sleep, when to move, and so on.

Some yearlings are especially hard to discourage and may hang around the mother all summer. Others soon leave and either take up a solitary existence or form an association with other moose—often with older bulls. This relationship is more common for yearling bulls than for yearling females. Apparently young moose are so accustomed to the leadership of older animals that they gladly follow the bulls. Surprisingly, mature bulls are quite tolerant of the yearlings. Sometimes the expelled youngsters meet other rejected ones and form juvenile bands.

As the gestation period of 240 to 246 days (Peterson, 1966) nears its end, the pregnant cow hunts for a secluded spot. Preferred places are islands of dense tree cover or shrubs surrounded by openings,

Calving country along the Green River, in western Wyoming.

with abundant spring forage nearby. Most calves, whether in Alaska or Wyoming, are born in late May and early June. Some variation has been noted, however. One captive cow gave birth to a calf on May 7. James Hatter in his study of the moose of British Columbia (1950) reported a February sighting of a cow moose accompanied by a calf that was "no larger than an average September animal." Although the size of the animal could possibly be attributed to some reason other than a late birth date, it is probable that this calf was born in the fall rather than in the spring.

A cow's first birthing usually produces a single calf; after that twins are born about 15 per cent of the time. Twinning rates vary greatly throughout the range and are believed to be influenced by the quantity and quality of the available food. Triplets are quite rare. The ratio of male calves to female calves is about 50:50.

Cows with twins seem unconcerned about the welfare of the second youngster as long as one of them is nearby. Sometimes when both twins are captured simultaneously for tagging, the cow will leave with the calf that is released first.

Newborn calves are reddish-brown with a paler head, dark eye rings, and a dark muzzle. The characteristic moose nose and flexible upper lip are not yet developed. They have very short necks. They are not spotted, as are elk calves and deer fawns; they weigh from 22 to 35 pounds, stand from 27 to 35 inches at the shoulder, and are about 40 inches long (Moyle, 1965). Calves are born with their eyes open and an hour or so after birth may nurse for the first time. Awkward and wobbly during the next few days, they do little but rest and nurse.

However, there are times when the strength of an hours-old calf is truly amazing. One early June day a few years ago, I was driving along the upper reaches of Wyoming's Green River about 8 miles from where the river runs out of Green River Lakes. This is high, open country with dense patches of willow and bright aspen groves.

This moose calf is not more than three days old.

It is a favorite calving area for moose, although when I was there the weather had been unusually warm and many of the pregnant cows had apparently moved into higher country. I didn't see as many as I had expected.

Finally I saw a cow standing beside a clump of willows along the bank of Green River. It looked like a good calving spot, and she seemed unusually alert. I wasn't too anxious to get close to her, since there were no climbable trees within a quarter of a mile; so I approached cautiously. She didn't run—an indication that a calf was nearby. This proved to be true. Through my binoculars I could see that she had not yet been able to eliminate all the afterbirth. A calf only minutes old, I was certain, lay hidden in the willow thicket. I wanted very much to get a picture of a newborn moose. Sometimes a cow moose with a very young calf has not yet had time to form as strong an attachment for it as she will at a later date, and often runs a few hundred yards away if approached by a man. Since it was pretty certain that the calf would be too weak to run and wouldn't know I was an enemy anyway, I waved my arms and yelled at the cow. She was not anxious to leave but finally did so, walking about 25 yards down the river bank before stopping and looking back at me and then at the clump of willows. When I shouted again and edged closer, she moved off another 25 yards. Then I saw the tiny red-brown calf floundering along after her, its still-wet hair glistening in the sunlight. I immediately returned to the car, thinking that my departure would encourage the cow to stop, for the calf was much too young and weak to be following the cow through the river bottom.

I drove back down along the river to where it curved in toward the road. In the bend of the stream there was a dense willow thicket in which fifty moose could easily have hidden. I was certain that the cow and her new calf would be there; instead, I found her standing by the side of the road. I stopped the car, and she crossed in front. A few yards behind, the little one staggered gamely along. Watching the

This cow moose was upset because I was near her calf.

Apparently moose calves rarely flatten themselves on the ground to hide as this one was doing.

mother start up a steep sidehill, I thought the baby would never make it. It would wobble upward a few feet and then stagger backward, but eventually it disappeared with its mother in the timber. I doubt that the calf was more than two hours old; yet in about twenty minutes' time it had traveled at least 500 yards over rough terrain and topped it off by climbing a steep hill.

Unlike the female elk and deer, the cow moose does not feed far from her calf. Nor does the baby flatten itself on the ground and lie motionless for long periods of time. It generally lies on one side with its legs either stretched out or folded under the body. It may rest its chin on the ground but most often holds its head up with ears cocked and constantly twitching.

The cow moose is very protective, so much so that anything—man, beast, or machine—is in danger of immediate attack if it approaches her calf too closely.

On page 55 is a photograph of the only moose calf that Jim Straley has ever seen in all his years of working with moose that hid by flattening out on the ground and remaining motionless. The youngster had traveled a long way and was obviously very tired.

Straley has tagged many moose calves during his years with the Wyoming Game Commission and has had many narrow escapes from irate mother moose. He refuses to get close to a calf unless there is a climbable tree nearby. His tagging technique is to run toward the cow yelling at the top of his lungs. Usually she trots off 100 yards or so and watches. This gives the tagging team time to grab the calf, which usually is not afraid, and pop a tag painlessly into its ear.

Once in a while the cow does not stay away long enough, and then there is a race for the car or a tree or whatever else is close that a moose cannot climb into or up. On a few memorable occasions, Straley and his fellow workers had to spend the better part of the day in a tree while an angry moose patrolled the ground below.

The mother moves slowly so that her youngster can follow her easily.

Straley does most of his tagging of moose calves during the last week of May and the first week of June. After that, he says, the calves are too fast for a man to catch.

After two or three days the calf is strong enough to follow the cow about but is apt to tumble over logs or get caught in the brush. Cows show a definite consideration for their young by moving slowly and avoiding difficult obstacles such as streams and rocks. It is probable that for several months the cow remains within a mile or so of the place where the calf was born.

While the cow feeds, the calf may rest nearby. Strange noises or an

A calf beds down after feeding.

intrusion by another animal causes the cow to look in the direction of the calf to see if it is safe. Research workers seeking calves for tagging or examination have taken advantage of this habit to locate them. Should the intruder be another moose passing too near the calf, the cow will approach with ears folded back, mane erected, and head outstretched. She may rear up on her hind legs and paw the air with her forefeet. The warning is obvious and few animals care to challenge a cow moose. Should the warning not be sufficient, the angry female strikes with her heavy front feet. This is usually enough to discourage even an overcurious bull or a prowling bear.

Cows with calves retreat from a danger area slowly, with frequent stops for a look in the direction of the disturbance. Sometimes the calf runs ahead, pausing every 30 yards or so to wait for the cow. Or the calf may stay alongside the cow or fall behind. Sometimes the calf matches the "alert" pose of the cow, standing broadside, with ears cocked and head held high, while it, too, looks toward the disturbance.

Some cows are so fearless in protecting their calves that tagging crews in Alaska were amazed when cow moose reared and struck with their front hoofs at the hovering helicopter.

Calves grow rapidly on a rich diet of mother's milk and during the first month gain from 1 to 2 pounds each day. In three weeks they double their weight. In its second month the calf begins sampling browse and gains from 3 to 5 pounds daily.

Generally, cows nurse their calves in some secluded place; therefore, nursing is not often seen. Cows have been known to call to their young at feeding time; it appears that usually the calf comes to meet the cow.

In "The Social Integration of the Moose Calf" (1958), Margaret Altmann states: "The moose cow frequently has to squat low or lie down so that the calf may be able to reach the udder."

Nursing periods in five observed instances averaged thirty-five to fifty seconds. Rollin H. Denniston (1956) described a nursing period

59

that lasted for three and one half minutes, with the hungry calf butting vigorously at the udder all the while. Twin calves may nurse simultaneously. To end the nursing period the cow steps away.

It is not known how much a calf in the wild consumes at each nursing, but a captured female calf believed to be two weeks old drank a quart of half-strength evaporated milk three times a day. The quantity was gradually increased until it reached 2 gallons a day when the calf was nine weeks old. Another orphaned moose calf at five weeks of age was drinking 2 quarts of a condensed-milk-and-water mixture three times a day. It seems likely that calves in the wild take in less milk at a feeding but nurse more often.

After feeding and cavorting about, calves return to brush or high grass and bed down. The cow does not at any time "hide" the calf, which always exercises a free choice of where it wishes to rest. Its partial or complete concealment against discovery is aided by the indifference of the cow. When she finishes eating, she may go to the calf and nuzzle, lick, or sniff it. The youngster may then rise and follow its mother.

Calves are taught to swim at an early age. Probably the cow leads the calf first into shallow streams or ponds, relying upon the youngster's strong instinct to follow to get it into this new and strange element. Next, she probably gets the little one into deeper water where it must swim. Sometimes this takes several tries, but eventually the calf is almost as much at home in the water as it is on land.

A calf judged to be less than a week old was seen to follow its mother in a 100-yard swim between two islands. It was a long journey for the baby, which reported its distress to its mother with a high-pitched bleating. She encouraged the struggling youngster with low-pitched grunts. It took the calf about seven minutes, but it made the crossing successfully. Twelve hours later the pair made the return journey.

Calf mortality is greatest during the first two weeks after birth. In an Alaskan study this was determined to be between 22 and 26 per

This calf follows its mother into a shallow stream.

It's time to think about investigating the world.

cent. Mortality of twin calves was higher than that of single calves. This was due, no doubt, to the difficulty of producing strong twins on the usually meager winter diet. Some calves are in poor physical condition at birth, and a spell of cold, wet weather during the parturition (birthing) period lowers their chances of survival. Drowning seems to be fairly common. Calves may become tangled in brush or accidentally kicked by the mother. Predation by bears is also a factor, but it does not seem to be widespread.

Calves that survive these early hazards gain strength in the growing warmth that leads to summer and a widening introduction to the fascinating world around them.

Summer is a time for loafing—and yawning.

Summer

SUMMER IS the quiet season for moose—a time without strain or pressures. In the spring there are new calves to worry about. Fall brings the tensions and disruptions of the rutting season. And in winter the search for minimum food requirements is constant. Summer, on the other hand, is a resting time, a vacation from the rigorous demands of the remainder of the year.

The worst thing that normally happens to a moose in summer is being constantly annoyed by flies and mosquitoes. Otherwise, their lives seem devoted to nothing more exciting than eating, sleeping, and loafing.

Cows with calves continue their solitary existence. The calf shows a greater restlessness, but the mother's protective vigil is not relaxed.

Bulls are basically "loners" during the summer but do not particularly avoid other moose. They just ignore one another unless their casual grazing activities bring them too close, and then one bull may drive another one away. A yearling was seen to be so treated, but after it ran a distance of about 5 yards the larger animal became indifferent. Bulls are often seen near feeding cows, yearlings, and other bulls, but their association is tenuous at best. No obvious leaders or dominant animals emerge when such a grouping occurs, and the animals come and go independently. In Alaska it was noted that when these aggregations were disturbed, the individuals generally moved off at the same rate and in the same direction.

During very warm periods moose seek out cool places and frequently enter lakes and ponds to feed on succulent aquatic plants. Higher elevations with beaver ponds, swampy lakes, or the headwaters of streams provide most of the things they need to make the summer comfortable.

Young calves often run and jump about in what appears to be a form of play, and three-month-old calves have been seen beating at low brush with their heads, emulating a behavior pattern shown by males in rut. Adult moose have also been observed indulging in playlike actions. A yearling bull with his antlers still in velvet was seen to run several times at a small willow clump, but he veered off each time just as he reached it. After that he repeatedly slipped one antler under a small bunch of twigs and tossed it.

I watched a yearling female play in the water near a young bull. She faced the bull at a distance of about 10 feet and pawed at the water with a forefoot. Water flew for 30 feet in all directions, thoroughly soaking the young bull, but he seemed to like it. When he started toward the female, she turned with a derisive toss of her head and trotted off through the shallow water, splashing with abandon. Obviously she was enjoying herself.

Bulls with antlers still in velvet occasionally spar for a few seconds at a time but take extreme care not to injure their growing antlers. Two yearling cows were watched as they feinted an attack, but they soon ended the "play" by running off a few yards. Play periods always seem to be brief.

When danger threatens, or seems to, a calf usually acts quite indifferent. Apparently it is so confident of its mother's protection that it leaves the detection of sources of danger and evasive or defensive action entirely up to her. This dependency upon the cow is so strong that yearlings develop protective habits rather slowly and probably somewhat reluctantly. Occasionally they act amazingly tame around people.

A yearling cow plays in the water—and splashes a young bull.

Food is abundant and life is good in the summertime.

During the summer the hair lengthens and tends to become lighter in color, more reddish- or grayish-brown. By September the pelage is long and thick and the animal is again ready for winter. This cold-weather coat is of long coarse guard hairs, 5 to 6 inches long on the neck and shoulders, with a fine woolly underfur. It is almost an inch thick over the back, with a cellular structure that gives the animal protection from the cold.

I have found no records of pure melanism or albinism in moose. Melanism, the all-black phase, could easily be overlooked because the normal coloring is so dark. An all-white animal, on the other hand, would be quite noticeable—and would be obvious to predators, which may be why so few albinos have been seen.

Summer

Some white, or very light-colored, moose have been reported. A completely white moose—an antlered cow bearing single spikes—was shot in Ontario in 1963 but was determined not to be a pure albino because her eyes were dark. In the September 1962 issue of *Outdoor Life,* Lee Wulf reported seeing a white bull moose in Newfoundland and included color photographs of the animal. However, this, too, was an incomplete albino. There were a few flecks of brown on the skin plus a hand-sized patch of brown on the shoulders, and the eyes were brown.

The daily routine of moose follows a fairly simple pattern. They become active before dawn and feed until midmorning. Then most

The daily routine is fairly simple. After a morning feeding period, moose take a midday rest.

of them bed down for a rest period that may last as long as six hours. Their main feeding periods are in the early morning and the late evening. However, some moose can be seen feeding at any hour of the day. The second big activity period begins between four and five in the afternoon and lasts until after dark. The extent of after-dark activity is somewhat unclear. It appears that during the summer moose may travel quite a bit at night.

One researcher was fortunate enough to have a cow spend the night near his front door, and he was thus able to record her activities. She appeared at 11:30 P.M., fed for fifteen minutes, and then lay down. She dozed and chewed her cud until 2:30 A.M., when she got up and fed again for ten minutes. There was another period of resting, and at 4:50 A.M. the cow got up and walked away. A month later, possibly the same cow stayed near the house and during the night fed three times and went to a different bed location after each feeding.

The moose is primarily a browser, eating mostly the leaves, twigs, and branches of woody plants. It prefers the tender stems of the most-recent growing seasons but when necessary will crop older growth up to a half-inch in diameter.

Frederick F. Knowlton, in his study of moose in Montana, reported their summer foods to be 70.6 per cent forbs, 28.6 per cent browse, and 0.6 per cent grass and grasslike plants.

The mainstay of the moose diet is willow, but it also eats other trees, both coniferous and deciduous, along with herbaceous plants, aquatic plants, and grass and grasslike plants. The amounts and kinds vary in different localities, depending upon the plants that are present and their palatability.

Moose also eat the bark from poplar, aspen, willows, alder, mountain ash, striped maple, shad bush, fire cherry, and red maple, using their teeth to scrape it off the tree trunks. Bark-eating seems to reach a peak when the sap is rising in the spring, before the trees leaf out. I have watched Shiras moose "barking" aspen in Wyoming in late

Marks left by a moose on an aspen tree.

May. The amount of other forage available convinced me that the animals were eating the bark by choice.

Moose enjoy eating mushrooms, lichens, various ferns, sedges, grasses, horsetail, wild parsnip, brush honeysuckle, and large-leaf aster when these are available.

It has been reported that because moose have short necks and long legs they sometimes have to spread their legs or kneel down to feed on low-growing plants. I have never seen this. Several feeding moose that I have photographed were able to reach ground plants without difficulty. However, most of them had one foot ahead of the other—a stance that enabled them to lower their heads sufficiently. Captive moose that were fed from pans placed directly on the ground had no problem and did not bend their forelegs while feeding.

This yearling cow feeds on ground cover without kneeling. Her half-step forward may be necessary in order for her to reach the ground.

Moose also feed extensively on the roots, tubers, and tender leaves of aquatic plants whenever they can. Their amazing ability to find these underwater plants reflects a remarkable degree of sensitivity—apparently to touch. Moose have frequently been observed to dive completely under and come up with a mouthful of pondweed, even though no part of the plants is visible on the surface.

They can submerge their heads for up to sixty seconds, although the time is usually shorter. Adolph Murie reported that Isle Royale moose kept their heads under for a minute and a half several times. They get their mouths full and then lift their heads out of the water to swallow. When feeding continuously the animals reach underwater again in about five seconds. This is a noisy activity because water cascades off their heads and, in the case of bulls, their antlers each time they are lifted.

A moose feeds on aquatic plants in shallow water.

Moose have been known to dive to submerged vegetation in water over 18 feet deep. Sometimes when they go that deep, not a ripple remains to show where they went down. It often appears that in deep water they have trouble staying under. The rump may float to the surface, or they may roll to one side. They also feed on floating plant life while swimming.

When undisturbed, a moose feeds on aquatics for thirty minutes to an hour at a time. Some have been seen to recess for ten or fifteen minutes and then return to the water for another feeding period.

Some of the moose's favorite aquatic plants are yellow pond lily, sweet-scented water lily, wild celery, wild rice, pondweeds, and water shield. Rollin H. Denniston (1956) observed Wyoming moose entering ponds to feed extensively on algae.

The extent of aquatic plants in the summer diet seems to be much greater in eastern North America than in Montana and Wyoming, where it is estimated to be less than 10 per cent. Along toward the latter part of August, aquatic feeding diminishes as the plants reach maturity and become tough and unpalatable.

When browsing, moose mostly prefer leaves, but in fall and winter they eat twigs. In some places—Jackson Hole, for example—99 per cent of their diet was browse from about November 16 to April 15.

In browsing, the moose either "nips" or "strips." Nipping, which is most common, consists of grasping terminal twigs between the lower incisors and the premaxillaries of the upper jaw. (The moose has no upper incisors.) With a quick upward jerk of its head, it breaks off the twig. When stripping, which is done only when plants are leafed out, the moose grasps the branches a foot or so from the end and with a sidewise movement of its head pulls the branch through its mouth and strips off all the leaves and small lateral shoots. Sometimes the moose removes leaves down to the tip and then nips off the terminal bud.

More than 50 per cent of all browsing is at a level between 2 and 4

Moose-browsed willow tips are frequently found 12 feet above the ground.

feet above the ground. When necessary a moose can reach upward 9 to 10 feet for food. Browsing signs 12 feet high are common, but this is believed to result from winter browsing, when packed snow provides a platform for the animal to stand on.

74

Moose droppings reflect the seasonal changes in diet. In summer, owing to the high moisture content in their feeds, the excrement is a soft, formless mass similar in appearance to that of domestic cattle. Winter droppings are distinct pellets, rounded and elongated, up to 1¾ inches long, which look like compressed sawdust. The winter diet of dry, woody browse accounts for this. In the spring and fall, droppings have the pellet form but are not so dry.

When undisturbed and food is plentiful, moose move about very little, leaving their feeding places only to drink. Some individuals remain in the same clump of willows for as long as two weeks. They move slowly through the brush, covering only a few yards during a feeding period. If frightened at the beginning of the feeding, moose move to a different spot before they resume.

Mature bulls are the most intense about their feeding. They may sample nearby plants while traveling but generally move to a feeding place and concentrate on that for a long period of time. In an Alaskan study most of the bulls observed fed for at least an hour, but one extremely hungry individual fed for 116 minutes without stopping.

Yearlings, probably still affected by the abrupt termination of their close association with their mothers, feed more or less at random during the summer. They lack the alertness of older animals and are often noisy in their movements. They wander about without apparent purpose, feeding first in one spot and then in another. By the end of summer they have become independent of their mothers and concentrate more on their feeding.

Cows with calves are the most alert of all and frequently assume an attentive position while chewing or swallowing just-gathered food. Their feeding periods average a little more than an hour.

When cows feed on aquatics, their calves lie down on shore. Every fifteen to thirty minutes the youngsters swim out to their mothers, nuzzle for a few minutes, and then return to dry land. As they get older, they browse along the shore opposite the feeding cows.

Calves begin to browse in early summer.

Although calves begin their browsing in early summer, they don't spend a long of time at it, averaging about a half-hour in every feeding period. They pick individual leaves or strip small bunches from the ends of branches. Occasionally, a calf feeds on aquatic plants, but at this early age it does not normally submerge the entire head.

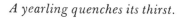

A yearling quenches its thirst.

Mature moose eat between 50 and 60 pounds of food a day in summer.

A mature moose requires a lot of food to keep going. Various studies, including the feeding of captive moose, indicate that a full-grown animal eats between 40 and 50 pounds of browse a day in the winter and from 50 to 60 pounds a day in the summer. The larger amount in summer is believed to represent the additional moisture in the more leafy summer browse. This totals a monthly consumption of between 1,200 and 1,500 pounds of browse, which is more than the average moose weighs.

By comparison, white-tailed deer eat 10 to 12 pounds of food a day; elk, about 21 pounds; and a pronghorn, which weighs a tenth as much as a moose, 4½ to 5½ pounds daily.

In his study of the moose of central British Columbia, James Hatter related this browse consumption to a particular sample of winter range. He assumed a 50 per cent utilization as the proper use factor and calculated that it would require 198 acres a month of this particular winter range to provide the browse required for one moose. This adds up to a need for nearly 2 square miles of that range to see each moose through the winter. This, of course, only applies to the sample range with which Hatter worked. Other places might contain a great deal more food, or possibly less.

Like other herbivores, moose are attracted to what are commonly called salt licks. This is perhaps a misnomer, since the common table variety of salt, sodium chloride, which is normally thought of when the term "salt lick" is used, may not be the essential ingredient. Other mineral compounds are found in these licks which may be the important ones for moose. It is probably more appropriate to call them "mineral licks." Bulls, cows, and yearlings use licks; calves rarely, if ever, do. Licks are most popular in late spring and early summer and seldom used in winter.

Mineral licks can be either earth with a high mineral content or mineral springs. Through the effects of constant animal visits, seeping mineral springs often become little more than trampled mud holes. The earth of dry licks is eaten away by animals eager for the mineral salts contained in the soil. An Alaskan mineral lick was described as a big bare field that had been eaten down several feet.

There are occasional sparring matches between cows around licks. Both animals, their muzzles held high, rear up and strike out with their front feet. Rarely is there any contact. They simply paw the air. After such a display one usually leaves.

Bulls meeting at a lick seem to do little more than acknowledge each other's presence with a token nudge or two of halfhearted sparring.

Moose and white-tailed deer have been seen drinking beside one another from the waters of a lick. The moose appeared to ignore the deer.

Summer

Moose visit a lick at any time of the day but seem to prefer early morning, evening, and night. In eastern Canada, daylight visitors were predominately yearling moose. Most of the night visitors made more than one trip to the lick. On the average a moose spends thirty minutes or less at a mineral lick, but sometimes they stay around much longer. Visits of up to an hour and a half have been reported. On one occasion two cows spent about three hours taking turns at a salt block.

When a moose has satisfied its appetite, it looks for a resting place. Beds are well defined and can be seen in snow or tall grass as roughly oval-shaped depressions. The variety of bed locations in muddy "pot holes," bogs, swamps, marshes, hillsides, grassy swales, timbered areas, and snow indicates no preference for a particular terrain or cover. However, some spots become favorites, at least temporarily, and there may be many bed forms in one small area. A moose may use the same bed form repeatedly or choose a different one in the same area each time. During hot weather moose often lie in water 2 to 6 inches deep.

Moose show no preference for a particular terrain or cover when bedding down.

Popular bedding places are recognizable by the many body forms and a characteristic odor, which has been described as a combination of Lysol, iodoform, and barnyard. It is a pretty heady mixture and often enables a person to locate a much-used bedding ground before the body depressions can be seen. It is thought that this smell results from the excreta in the surrounding area or the decomposition of urine, or both.

Sometimes two moose that have been feeding near each other may leave the feeding area at the same time and choose bedding sites close together. It appears that moose are influenced to some extent by the behavior of others nearby—possibly representing nothing more than a reminder that it is time to do something else.

A moose sometimes lies down where it finishes feeding. Or it may gradually work its way toward its bedding ground in the nearby woods or other cover; then, when it finishes feeding, it moves purposefully toward the bedding place.

The exact bed location is not as haphazard as it may at first appear. Most are chosen so that the animal is either completely or partly concealed and is able to make a quick getaway if danger threatens. I have seen many moose bedded down in willow clumps in such a way as to be hidden from the side most likely to be approached by visitors. Moose in Yellowstone National Park and Jackson Hole frequently choose spots near roads frequented by tourists who never know the animals are there. It is amazing how easily a 1,000-pound moose can disappear behind a relatively small clump of willows. Fallen timber also offers partial concealment during resting periods.

Cows with young calves up to about six weeks old—at least those that I have seen—bed down fairly close to their young, usually within 2 to 10 feet.

In July 1969, I came upon a cow and her calf bedded together along the outer edge of a thick patch of willows in the Snake River bottom in Jackson Hole. I was about 30 yards away and 30 feet

A calf settles down near its mother, and they rub noses.

above them. They were 8 feet apart, and both were facing away from me. They may not have known that I was there. On the other hand, moose in that area are accustomed to people, and it is quite possible that the cow was aware of my presence but did not consider me dangerous at that distance. I watched for ten or fifteen minutes, during which time the calf moved its head around several times in a restless manner, got up, stretched, and walked to a willow clump a few feet away. After nibbling at the willows for a minute or so, it returned to the cow and lay down so close they could rub noses, which it looked as if they did for several seconds.

81

I left to explore elsewhere and when I came back, approximately an hour later, they were gone. I moved to another high vantage point and saw what I am sure was the same cow, even though I could not see the calf. She was lying down but had moved about 20 yards from where I had first seen her. This new location was such that I had not been able to see her from the first observation point.

I sat on the hill for some time, not more than 100 feet from her. Except for her head, she was concealed by willows. She chewed her cud placidly, showing no interest in my presence even though I was clearly visible. It was getting along toward the evening feeding period, and after about thirty minutes she stood up. When she did, the calf which had been lying beside her all the time was revealed. The cow looked directly at me and then began to feed casually. The calf stood around acting bewildered. The cow fed slowly away, and after five minutes she and the youngster disappeared in the willows.

By late September, when calves are more independent, they may bed down 50 or 60 feet away from the cow. On one occasion, I watched a cow pursued by an amorous young bull run for a half mile and vanish into the brush. Her calf seemed unaware that she had left. I waited for almost two hours, but the cow did not return during that time. However, by the following day the cow and calf were back together.

One late September day I was perched on a sage-covered bench some 30 feet above a beaver pond, watching a mature bull that was bedded on the opposite side. It was about four in the afternoon. The bull's head was plainly visible, although from ground level I doubt that I could have seen him because of the screening brush. He gave me a casual look and that was about all the concern he expressed, but a cow that he was consorting with and her calf got up from the willows to inspect me. They had not been visible previously. The calf nursed for about thirty seconds. The cow sampled some of the nearby willow tips, and then they both lay down again.

The next day, while photographing the same bull, I managed, by exercising some rare stupidity, to get directly in his path when he was no more than 15 yards away. It was not a position that I relished being in with such an unpredictable animal, and this one had been traveling most of the morning hunting either for the cow he had been with the previous day or for another one. From the sound of his frustrated grunting, I was convinced he was in a foul mood.

He stopped when he saw me and waited, partially concealed by some willows. After considering the matter for thirty seconds—while I appraised the surrounding trees for the nearest climbable one— the bull did none of the things I expected or dreaded. He lay down! Even as close as I was and knowing where he was, I could no longer see him.

When a moose first lies down it remains alert for some time, possibly a half-hour or more. Then it relaxes and begins to chew its cud (ruminate). Moose have also been seen ruminating while standing, but this is confined mostly to rest periods. I have not counted the rate

A cow contentedly chews her cud behind a clump of willows.

of chewing of a mature moose, but one report mentions 82 strokes ("chews") a minute. I checked a four-month-old calf that was, according to my count, ruminating at the rapid rate of 120 times a minute. It was lying down with its eyes closed. Its ears were in almost constant motion. Flies were unusually bad at the time, and this no doubt accounted for the ear movement.

There is nothing quite so contented looking as a cud-chewing ungulate, of which the moose is one. One would have to conclude that cud-chewing is a pleasant pastime. It is also an important part of an involved digestive process. The moose crops its food rapidly and swallows it quickly, chewing it only enough to put it into swallowable form. The swallowed vegetation goes into the first compartment, or rumen, of a complicated four-compartment stomach. There it is acted upon by a rich flora of bacteria that prepare it for digestion. The action is continued in the second stomach compartment, the reticulum. The resultant pulp, called the "cud," is then returned to the mouth in conveniently sized amounts for leisurely chewing. When thoroughly rechewed, the cud is again swallowed and goes into the third and fourth stomach compartments, where it is broken down to provide nourishment.

Resting moose may put their heads back on their sides, with the muzzle resting on the flanks, and they may close their eyes and appear to sleep for several minutes at a time. Sometimes they take a few mouthfuls of sedge or low shrub while lying down. After a lengthy period of lying on one side, they may get up, stretch, and then lie down again on the opposite side. They yawn frequently.

Before ending a resting period a moose will indulge in some restful neck and leg stretching, with the neck and head extended full length and the muzzle pointed upward at a 45-degree angle. The legs may be stretched full length to one side or the front legs extended straight forward. Moose seem to enjoy stretching as much as people do.

84

Moose move along the edge of, or just inside, timbered areas for protection.

Despite the simplicity of moose's daily schedules, they can be drastically affected by adverse weather and other disturbances in which they have difficulty in hearing or picking up scent. Windy days, for example, appear to inhibit their movements, but following a cool, windy period they become unusually active.

When moose move, they demonstrate some rather interesting traits.

In Alaska, cows with calves move along the edge of spruce and willow islands and fingers of tree growth. Sometimes they go along the edge, at other times just inside the edge of the timber. With willows partially screening them on one side and the dark background of the timber on the other, they are most difficult to see. When traveling toward open areas, moose use the long timber fingers stretching out into the openings to provide protection and concealment for as long as possible.

They do not seem to be impressed by the hazards of mud holes or bogs and tackle them without hesitation. When the going gets tough they stop to rest but apparently do not panic and start to flounder. Some do get stuck and perish, however.

As might be expected of an animal that feeds extensively on aquatic plants and learns to swim at an early age, mature moose become powerful and confident swimmers. Swimming speed has been estimated at 6 miles an hour, but even more remarkable is the endurance they have demonstrated by swimming up to 12 miles. It takes a good canoeist to keep up with one. Moose are not easily di-

Moose can swim at 6 miles an hour, for as long as two hours at a time.

verted from their original course when swimming, and unless something actually blocks their way, such as a boat, they will not turn aside. Their confidence in their swimming ability is also their undoing at times, and some are drowned in turbulent rivers or lost through thin ice.

After emerging from the water a moose shakes itself to get rid of the excess moisture. It stands with hind legs slightly spread and neck and head held parallel to the ground. The hair on neck, withers, and rump is raised, and the shake commences with the head and works its way back. I watched a big bull shake himself after swimming across the Yellowstone River and was amazed at the amount of water on the animal. For a moment or so he completely disappeared in the spray.

There appear to be many opinions as to when moose calves are weaned, ranging all the way from August to November. A captive moose calf was completely weaned by August 15, which indicates that moose calves do not need to depend upon their mothers for food much beyond that time, regardless of how long they actually nurse, which sometimes is unusually prolonged. Near Pelican Creek in Yellowstone National Park late one September, I saw a spike bull grazing alongside what I presumed was its mother and trying to nurse. It maintained contact for a few seconds before the female terminated the session, but I was unable to determine if any milk was actually ingested by the young bull.

A few days earlier, I observed a calf nurse for half a minute and then finish its meal with a few mouthfuls of willow leaves and twigs. During the nursing period the cow appeared to lift her leg slightly in order to help the large calf reach the udder.

As the summer months pass, there is a great change in the appearance of the calves. The reddish-brown calf coat is gradually replaced with a new one of dark grayish-brown, with a silvery cast over

By September, a moose calf looks like a junior edition of its mother.

the shoulders and neck. The face is brown and the legs a much lighter brown. Now the calf is much the same color as its mother.

Summer

It has been said that no other animal in America grows as rapidly as the moose. In relative comparison of weight gained by young to its adult size, this might not be true, but in pounds gained per day or month it probably is. Based on the growth of captive calves, which show considerable variation, weight of the youngster at summer's end would range from 150 to 250 pounds. This is a gain of from 115 to 215 pounds in about three and one-half months. Growth is slower during the winter, but by the time the calves are a year old they weigh from 400 to 600 pounds (Peterson, 1955). A two-year-old bull weighs about 700 pounds; a three-year-old, about 900 pounds (Hosley, 1949). A cow weighs slightly less and reaches about 600 pounds at two years and 600 to 800 pounds when mature (Hosley, 1949).

The face of the calf elongates considerably during the first six months, but the overhanging muzzle or "muffle" does not usually reach full development until after the first year.

A bull searching for a cow.

Autumn

AGAINST THE low morning sun, the great bull moose was a silhouette striding through the frost-coated willows. Sunlight glinted from each icy crystal and spotlighted the palms of the moose's wide multi-pointed antlers. With every other step he grunted—urgently, emphatically. From behind the concealing white trunks of a gold-topped aspen grove some distance away stepped a cow moose, trailed by a four-month-old calf. She answered his call. It was the first day of autumn. The rutting season was in full swing.

For the past month or so subtle changes had shown in the actions and attitudes of all but the calves, gradually building toward the tense, highly emotional state of the moose that exists during the rut.

By the end of August moose are in their best physical condition of the year. Juveniles, especially young bulls, express their reaction to the mounting sex drive by increased excitability, restlessness, and irritability. Among groups of these youngsters there is much sparring, kicking, and running about. Those that have spent the summer as self-appointed associates of tolerant old bulls find them less tolerant and quickly learn to avoid the now ill-tempered mature animals. Young bulls are harassed and driven away by older bulls, and juvenile females get a similar treatment from the cows, which apparently consider them rivals for the attentions of the males.

This leads to the formation of groups of from two to five young animals which may be joined by other unattached moose. They feed together, though often widely spaced, and move more or less in unison—sometimes even in single file. Most of the members of these groups are young bulls, and mock battles between them are frequent. They move about more than solitary moose, but they avoid the big bulls in rut and the mating groups.

Prerutting activity of the mature bulls seems to start with the shedding of the antler velvet. Contests, more or less of a practice nature, take place between bulls, with the two contestants carefully placing their antlers together and engaging in a shoving match.

The antlers, often festooned with dangling streamers of loosened velvet, are rubbed against trees—probably to relieve an itch—or are thrashed about in mock battles with brush. This has the effect of stripping away the drying velvet and, presumably, preparing the bull for the serious business of the rut to follow.

Usually by mid-September the mature bull begins searching for a single cow in oestrus, or sexual heat; males do not gather large harems as do elk. Instead, they associate with one cow at a time in a form of limited polygamy. The bull moose is an ardent mate for as long as the heat period of the female lasts—usually seven to ten days. Then he

A bull chasing a cow.

leaves her in search of another. In the meantime females in oestrus do not wait around to be found but also go looking for a mate.

Two tagged males in Jackson Hole, Wyoming, were observed with three females each in an eleven- to fourteen-day period.

Various studies indicate that most moose breed between September 15 and October 15. From their study on the reproduction of moose in British Columbia, R. Y. Edwards and R. W. Ritcey concluded that the oestrous cycle of moose occurs four times a year—in early September, in late September through early October, in late October, and in late November. Their study also indicates that about 89 per cent of the conceptions take place during the second period—late September through early October.

However, there are some rather interesting variations from this normal situation. In Quebec on August 14 a calf was discovered that was only a few hours old. This would suggest a successful mating about the previous December 15.

On December 17, 1969, I followed a group of moose for several hours, taking pictures of their winter feeding. There were 12 to 18 inches of snow on the ground. The temperature was 27 degrees. There was no wind, and it was a beautiful clear day. The group was composed of five animals—a mature bull, two young bulls that were probably three-and-a-half years old, with small palms in their antlers, and a cow and a calf. The group moved rather compactly and with more cohesion than would be expected in a casual encounter. It was a puzzling situation until I saw the mature bull, his head held high, approach the cow and test her. A few seconds later he attempted to mount, but she would not accept him. This action was not repeated during the several hours that I watched them, but there was enough serious rutting behavior to suggest the reason for the grouping: a late oestrous cycle in the cow.

The female calls the bull in a drawn-out wail that has been described as *wuow-wuow-wuow*. If there is a bull within hearing distance, the cow usually gets a prompt response. The male's reply is a rather deep-toned, sharply terminated grunt continuously repeated.

In Newfoundland, bull moose eager to find lovesick females have mistaken the moaning horns of diesel trains for their calls. Sometimes, in their eagerness, the running bulls collide with the trains.

Having found a mate, the bull tests her readiness by sniffing her genital organs. This may be followed by a head-high pose in which the bull remains motionless with his upper lip curled back. A period of courtship that generally follows this first introduction may last for several days. During this time the bull follows the cow around, usually tagging along behind her. The cow's four-month-old calf remains a part of the breeding group but is more or less ignored by the bull.

The association proceeds until the cow will stand for mating. This may be repeated many times for a period of several days.

An unusual part of the rutting activity is the digging of wallows by moose, the purpose of which is somewhat obscure. I watched the entire procedure from the unsafe distance of 50 feet. There may have been reasons for the activity that I didn't recognize or understand, but it obviously created intense excitement in both bull and cow.

This episode took place in an extensive willow thicket near Jackson Lake in Jackson Hole, Wyoming. The breeding group consisted of a mature bull, a cow and calf, and a young bull with small palmated antlers. The young bull was obviously hoping to get the cow away from the larger male.

The ground was covered with heavy grass but had been softened by recent rain. The bull started digging with his front hoofs. He would dig four or five times with one foot and then change to the other. After several changes he stopped and urinated into the excavation. While this was going on the cow was standing to one side behind a willow screen, and the juvenile bull was in a similar position on the other side. The calf was not visible; I assumed it was bedded down somewhere nearby.

The bull changed positions often so that he dug in a different part of the wallow each time. He urinated frequently into the excavation. The cow got so excited she finally came out from behind the willows. She sniffed at the bull or the excavation—I could not be sure which, but the odors from both were probably fairly strong by this time.* The young bull, watching from a few yards away, also became greatly agitated and approached too close to the older male, which lunged at him. He managed to dodge the blow.

After approximately ten minutes of work on the wallow, the older bull gouged into the excavation with his antlers several times and then lay down. The cow could no longer contain herself and lay down beside him. Most often cows have been seen to force bulls out of wallows by striking them with their forefeet. Then they lie down in the wallow and roll and turn until they are covered with mud. Bulls may retaliate within a few minutes and use their forefeet to get the cows out.

When two belligerent cows find a fresh wallow, they may indulge in a sort of "king of the hill" contest to see who gets it. One may try to lie down in it, only to be beaten off by the other. Such encounters are usually between young and mature animals. The older animal with her calf will try to stay in the wallow with the youngster by her side. She may get up at intervals and chase the other cow away and then return to roll in the wallow. The bull stands by on such occasions but takes no part in the squabble.

In the wallow episode that I watched, the young bull came up within a few feet to investigate the bull and cow lying together in the wallow, and he even acted as if he wanted to get in with them. The

---

* *Editor's Note:* According to Bourlière (1964), in many mammals the odor of their urine is a powerful sexual stimulant preliminary to copulation. He cites it in the European red squirrel, the European wild rabbit, the American porcupine, and the moose. It is well known as a part of the mating ritual of the North American cottontails (*Sylvilagus*), whose sex habits have been much studied by American mammalogists.

A bull begins to dig a wallow.

He gouges his antlers into the excavation before lying in it.

The female cannot resist and joins him.

When a curious young bull comes too close, the older one chases him away.

big bull tolerated this for a few seconds and then got up and charged the trespasser, which left in one direction, unharmed; the cow went in another. The big bull then followed the cow.

I could hear noises in the willows but was unable to determine which of the animals was causing them or what the actions were. After about five minutes the young bull returned. He went directly to the wallow and lay down, but was quickly dissatisfied and got up. He dug a little more, rather halfheartedly, and lay down again. A few minutes later he got up and apparently followed the bull and cow.

The oval-shaped wallow was about 4 feet long, 2 to 3 feet wide, and 2 to 3 inches deep in the center. There was a strong smell about it. In this same area, in which, during three days of observation, I saw no other rutting groups, there were several other wallows as well as a number of bedding sites. The wallows were easily distinguishable from the bedding sites which showed no signs of digging. I had no opportunity to determine whether or not a wallow is used more than once. My observations tend to make me believe that they are not. The digging I saw seemed to be a spontaneous activity brought on by an emotional peak. It is hard to imagine that a rutting bull moose, excited by the presence of a willing cow as well as that of a competing bull, would spend time looking for a wallow he had dug the day before.

Two days earlier I had watched this same bull and cow—I think they were the same ones because of the photographs I have in which the antlers look the same—a quarter of a mile from where the wallow incident I just described occurred. From a high point I could see into the willows. A young bull (not the one described above) was apparently trying to steal the cow away. Much of the action was somewhat illogical from my point of view and didn't seem to fit accepted moose behavior. The young bull would be tolerated at quite close range; then, for some reason I could not detect, the larger bull would chase him away. There seemed to be some active aggression going on when I arrived. I didn't see it start, but the two bulls and the cow were moving about in the willows, probably hidden from one another by the willow clumps, but from my elevated position I could see all three animals. Their moves and countermoves reminded me of some strange three-handed checker game with new rules.

Eventually, the smaller bull got into the right spot relative to the cow and chased her away. They ran for possibly a half-mile; meanwhile it seemed to take the older bull several minutes to realize that they were gone. Eventually he trotted off in the same direction, following, I believe, their scent. I did not think he would find them easily, but in less than thirty minutes he was bringing the cow back.

Young bulls in particular are extremely restless during the rutting season—possibly because their small size virtually eliminates the chance of getting mates and releasing the built-up tensions of the rutting season. For almost two hours I watched a young bull that was bedded down in a timber patch alongside the Snake River. I was unable to tell whether or not he was lying in a wallow, but during the observation period he was seldom still for longer than ten minutes at a time. Several times he jumped suddenly from his bed and ran for 20 feet, as if startled by something. Finally I walked to where I knew he would see me, and I got no reaction at all. I concluded that whatever was making him restless was due to the rutting influence, not to my presence.

Young bulls are generally no threat to mature animals and, when challenged, retreat rather than fight. But if the challenging bull is approximately the same size and is willing to accept combat, a battle will ensue. The bulls approach each other with lowered heads, walking stiff-legged and determined. With ears laid back and manes bristling, the animals meet head on with a rattling of antlers. These fights are primarily shoving matches, with each animal striving to get the other off balance. One bull may gain a slight advantage and force the other to step backward. The yielding bull braces himself and regains the advantage or stalemates the contest. If one slips or stumbles or is simply overpowered, the other immediately strikes him in the ribs or flank. This is usually enough to bring about a decision, and the loser leaves. If neither gains an advantage, they discontinue the head-to-head attack but remain near each other as a constant threat. This can go on for days until one decides the tensions of this "cold war" are too much for him and leaves.

A few fights are to-the-death struggles; sometimes the antlers of the combatants become locked together, as happens to smaller deer, and both animals die.

During these fights the cow and her calf stand by, unperturbed by the battle and apparently unconcerned about the outcome.

Bull moose are generally considered to be dangerous and unpre-

I retreated from a position too close to a rutting bull.

dictable during the rutting season. During the autumn of 1969 in Jackson Hole, I heard several stories about nearby hikers who had been forced by irate bull moose to take to the trees. Since I was not present at these treeings, I have no opinions regarding the alleged attacks. However, during that period I confronted several bull moose at distances of from 25 feet to 25 yards, and none of them made any movements toward me. Two or three of them stopped what they were doing and looked as if they would have preferred me to be somewhere else, but that was all.

In the fall of 1967 I did see a moose tree a man in Yellowstone National Park. The treed individual will, I am sure, be quite surprised if he ever reads this, since he obviously had no idea there was anyone else around.

A companion, H. H. Griffin, of Portland, Oregon, and I had been prowling around the Pelican Creek area for two days looking for moose. I was trying to get pictures. Griffin, who had never seen moose before, was along just to observe. Early our first day we had located a couple of hungry yearlings that fed industriously while we moved to within 30 feet of them. They were interesting to watch, but what I really wanted to find was a big bull. Around nine o'clock the next morning one came out of the timber 100 yards south of the highway and began feeding in a patch of willows in the marsh through which Pelican Creek winds on its way to Yellowstone Lake. The boggy black soil prevented me from getting as close as I wanted to, so we waited. After feeding for some forty-five minutes, the bull moved back into the timber. We made a long hike around the edge of the marsh and came in behind the spot where the animal had disappeared. I moved slowly—I have been extremely cautious about such maneuvers ever since the time I circled to intercept a moving bull in thick timber and did it so well that he almost ran over me. This time I was luckier.

The bull had bedded down about 50 yards inside the timber and was contentedly chewing his cud when we saw him. He was a big one, coal black in the deep forest shadows, but his brush-polished antlers—an unusually fine set for a Shiras bull—seemed to glow in the dim light.

Griffin described him as looking like a "Volkswagen wearing an old-fashioned wooden porch swing."

While my friend stayed back out of the way, I inched cautiously forward. At 50 feet I stopped. The bull was showing no signs of hostility, but I was as close as I needed to be with the telephoto lens I was using. I checked the light with an exposure meter. It was really too dark for effective pictures, so I backed off, and after a short consultation, we decided to leave and come back later. The bull would, we thought, rest for several hours.

When we returned after lunch the animal was gone. We scouted around and finally glimpsed him through the trees, standing out in the water and accompanied by a cow. The bull turned and slowly waded in toward shore. A young man we had not seen jumped from where he had been crouched behind some shrubs and scrambled up a small evergreen tree.

I am sure that the man scratched himself badly going up the tree, for twigs were flying in all directions. I saw no action by the bull that warranted such precipitous tree-climbing, but something may have happened before we got there. To be on the safe side—always a good idea when wild animals are involved—Griffin and I moved back to a blown-down tree, which offered a safe and easy-to-reach haven in case the bull really was in a dangerous mood. For about twenty minutes the animal stood beneath the tree in which the young man perched, but made no threatening gestures. Finally the bull waded back out into the water. The young man immediately slid down the tree and left hurriedly.

We walked out to the edge of the water, and I took several photographs of the cow and bull, now 50 yards away. They didn't even acknowledge my presence with so much as a glance.

The bull may have threatened the young man, but at no time was there a sign of attack upon us. Although I approved of the young man's caution, I could not help thinking he had overreacted and that he was really in no danger at the time.

In 1968 I saw a charge by a large bull in the same area. The bull and a cow were feeding about 75 yards off the highway. In the general vicinity there were also three younger bulls and another cow. This may have had something to do with the shortness of the larger bull's temper.

A carload of young people, German college students I gathered from their speech, walked over near the bull and, as young people will under such circumstances, kept testing their bravery by getting closer and closer until finally the old moose, irritated by their rashness, lunged at them. It was not much of a charge, and the bull did not follow it up, but there was really no necessity to do so since the youths set new speed records getting back to their car.

After the bull had resumed his feeding I eased to within 30 to 40 yards—good 300-mm. telephoto range—and immediately began taking pictures. I could have stayed there all day had it not been for another young visitor, also anxious to demonstrate his bravery, who crawled up behind a tree within 10 feet of the bull and shoved a camera at him. At this the bull terminated his feeding, waded across a 50-yard-wide marshy spot and vanished into the timber.

I was on hand when an Alaskan bull challenged a hunter who had killed the bull's companion only a few minutes before. However, I think the challenge was due, not to that, but to general orneriness and the rutting season. This bull had left after the shooting but had returned thirty minutes later, pawing the ground and thrashing the low brush with his antlers. The hunter, a long-time Alaska resident and familiar with moose, let him approach to within 35 yards before he decided the bull might be seriously considering an attack. He started firing into the ground under the animal's tender nose—we could see the sand and small stones striking him. This must have hurt, but it was not until after the fourth shot that the animal turned and disdainfully stalked off down the hill.

It is likely that many so-called bull moose attacks are misinterpretations of their intentions. Nevertheless, they are big, powerful animals, and it is better to be safe in a tree when you discover the moose really was not going to attack you, than to stay on the ground and discover that it was.

Cow moose may be bred and become pregnant during their second autumn season, when they are about sixteen months old. Whether or not a cow breeds at this early age seems to depend a great deal on the food she eats her first winter. During a good winter the female calf may develop to the point where she will have breeding capabilities the following fall. Substantially all females over two years old breed and continue to do so most of their lives.

A cow moose in Sweden was reported to be still producing healthy calves at twenty-one years of age. She eventually became so vicious that she had to be destroyed.

Young bulls sixteen months old are capable of successful matings, but the older dominant males seldom permit them to do so. A pair of captive moose, mated when they were sixteen months old, produced a healthy calf. However, bull moose reach their prime breeding period from their sixth to tenth year.

By the end of the breeding period in late October cow moose are hale and hearty. Some even gain weight. But the bulls are in poor physical condition. They have traveled widely, eaten sparingly, and rested poorly. Their time has been fully occupied with the rigorous demands of ardent cows and the need for constant vigilance against acquisitive bulls. They may lose as much as 150 pounds during the rutting season.

In his book *North American Moose*, Randolph L. Peterson states:

"All available records indicate that normally less than one-half of the adult cows (two years of age or older) produce calves each year."

Studies in various areas tend to support this statement. The reasons for this low rate of reproduction are not clear. One possibility is that female calves during the first winter lack the nutrients necessary for them to produce calves during their second winter. It has also been suggested that selective hunting, such as for bulls only, creates a shortage of males during the peak oestrus period. This may be especially significant in view of the bull moose's tendency to consort with only one cow for a week or more at a time.

Most of the time a moose will walk rather than run. Much of its home country is composed of marshes, bogs, and extensive tracts of blown-down timber. It is country shunned by many other animals, but the long-legged, sure-footed moose plods through it with confidence.

The long-legged, sure-footed moose can cover a lot of ground in a hurry.

When on firm ground and in a hurry moose may break into a ground-eating trot. Only rarely do they gallop, although they can. Motor vehicles have paced moose, and speeds of 19, 22, 27, and 35 miles an hour have been reported. It is likely that the top speed can be maintained for only a brief period of time, but this is enough to enable a moose to reach the safety of timber or a brush thicket.

It is interesting that the top speed of both white-tailed deer and elk —animals that also inhabit rough brush and wooded terrain—is estimated at 30 to 35 miles an hour, roughly the same as that of moose. The pronghorn, on the other hand, which lives in open country and relies on speed rather than cover for protection, has a top speed of 50 to 60 miles an hour.

When some object blocks its line of travel, a moose seldom jumps over it, preferring instead to step over or, if it is too high for that, to walk around it. When there is no alternative to jumping, the moose rears up on its hind feet, puts its front feet over the barrier, and springs over in a sort of standing high jump.

Richard N. Denney, formerly a game biologist for the State of Colorado, reported that he and Jim Straley had watched a large bull moose walk up to a five-strand barbed-wire fence in 3 feet of snow and clear the fence, without so much as touching the wire, in an uphill, flatfooted jump. That is enough of a demonstration to indicate that whether a moose likes to jump or not, it certainly has the ability to do so.

The length of stride—the distance between the prints where the same foot strikes the ground—of an average-sized bull when walking measures between 42 and 68 inches. During a fast trot the stride will range between 90 and 106 inches.

Moose have always been eagerly sought by hunters. One animal furnishes a lot of meat along with a valuable hide and other usable items. It is still an important food item to some natives of the Far

To some hunters, moose is still an important food item.

North. Several years ago while on a trip to Alaska I talked to several people who had moved there from the "southern 48" and also considered a moose in the freezer a vital addition to their food supply. They always tried to get one to see them through the winter. However, much of the hunting now is trophy hunting. The bull's magnificent antlers are his undoing. A great many hunters are interested only in obtaining a highly desirable addition to their trophy collection as well as tangible proof of their hunting ability.

I was not able to obtain complete figures on the number of moose killed by hunters in Canada in recent years, but if the hunting success in the United States as reported by the Fish and Wildlife Service is an indication, the number would not be extremely large. For the United States the number reported for 1968 was:

Alaska	6,272
Idaho	53
Montana	460
New Hampshire	3
Utah	14
Wyoming	989
	7,791

Compared to the 1968 kill in the United States of other big game species—over 2,000,000 deer, 88,000 elk, 54,000 pronghorns, 33,999 caribou—a total of 7,800 moose does not amount to much.

The significance of this is, I think, that the range requirements of the moose, plus its antisocial inclinations, more or less preclude a large moose population even under optimum conditions.

Moose-hunting tactics vary with the type of country. In the eastern part of their range, where the land is relatively flat and/or heavily wooded, the hunter often calls them to him. This is effective only during the rutting season. The hunter or his guide uses a call made of birch bark rolled into a megaphone shape, or the call may be made through cupped hands. The sound is supposed to imitate that of an amorous cow and often will excite a bull enough to make it come to the caller.

Young bulls tend to lose some of their normal caution when they hear a call and may come plowing through the brush right to the hunter. I once watched an Alaskan guide bring a three-year-old bull up to within 20 feet of us with a couple of seductive calls through his cupped hands. When the young bull stuck his head out of the brush and saw our party instead of the cow he expected, he was, if I am any judge of animal expressions, the most disappointed moose in Alaska. Old bulls are more wary. They circle for scent and approach noiselessly to see what is making the noise. They may spend a long time—perhaps hours—getting in close. Late evening and night seem to be the best times for calling.

Bulls may also be brought within gun range by rattling old antlers or sticks, or by breaking brush. This noise appears to interest them as being made by another bull, a probable competitor, thrashing his antlers about in the brush.

Moose are often hunted from canoes, sometimes in combination with calling, sometimes just by paddling silently along waterways with the expectation of eventually surprising one feeding in the water or along the shore.

In the West, where moose live in more mountainous country, stalking them is the preferred hunting method. A moose is big and dark enough to be seen easily a long distance away. If the sun is shining, the light-colored palms of his antlers flash in the sun like a heliograph and signal his presence. After a bull is located, the hunter and his guide study him carefully through binoculars or a high-powered spotting scope. Trophy hunters are interested in large antlers, record size if possible. Residents of moose country who hunt for the meat want younger animals. In either case a careful appraisal through the spotting scope enables them to decide if the stalk is worth while.

I have never killed a moose, nor do I have any desire to. However, I have been along as a photographer on several moose hunts and have seen several of the animals killed. On one of these occasions the hunter and I were somewhere near the Susitna River, about an hour's flight north of Tazlina Glacier in south-central Alaska. We were waiting on a grassy knoll above what was supposed to be a caribou pass. We didn't see any caribou, which is what we were looking for, but after about three hours two bull moose came up over the hill and began feeding about 200 yards below us. The area was devoid of trees, and it seemed a bit out of character for moose to be there. The hunter, Ted Van Thiel, then of Anchorage, Alaska, had a moose-hunting license in addition to one for caribou, and as they were both good bulls, the caribou hunt suddenly turned into a moose hunt.

We crawled across the face of the hill until we put a shoulder of it between us and the moose. There was almost no wind, but the occasional cool touch of it was right in my face as we crept down-ward, which meant the animals could not smell us. The shape of the hill gradually changed until we ran out of cover about 100 yards from the moose. This was practically point-blank range for the rifle, but I wanted to be closer for the photographs.

We inched our way back across the face of the hill to a spot directly above and 25 yards closer to the two animals. We were in plain sight, but they showed no signs of being aware of our presence. I got my pictures, and Van Thiel picked the largest of the two bulls and dropped him with one shot.

The next morning we climbed back to the place where we had left the skinned and quartered animal. With us was a young employee of the Fish and Wildlife Service who had been hunting in the area for a week before our arrival but had not yet seen a moose. As we got close we saw what we thought was a grizzly bear that had discovered the moose carcass and was camped on it. A check through binoculars showed it to be another large bull moose. He was lying down less than 100 yards from the moose carcass.

I followed the young man as he stalked to within 50 yards of the resting animal. While he was nervously getting ready to fire at his first moose, the animal saw us and stood up. He seemed undecided about what to do. While he was trying to make up his mind, the young man shot him.

These were easy hunts and probably unusual in that respect. Two other moose hunts I've been on, unarmed, were much tougher. In each instance the chosen quarry was from 1 to 2 miles away, and it

The young Alaskan hunter prepares to shoot his first moose.

took a slow and tiresome hike of several hours over the lumpy Alaskan muskeg, plus wading several icy streams and some arduous climbing, to get within gun range.

My somewhat meager observations of moose hunts suggest that, despite their size, moose are fairly easy to kill. Each of the animals described above was dropped in his tracks with one shot from a .270 caliber rifle firing 130 grain bullets. This is considered light, high-speed ammunition. Jack O'Conner, hunting editor of *Outdoor Life* maga-

Antlers gleaming in the sun signaled the presence of this mighty bull.

zine, has expressed a similar opinion regarding the ease with which moose are killed.

Once the moose is dead, the hard work starts. Dressing, skinning, and quartering an animal weighing from 1,000 to 1,800 pounds while it is lying on the ground or in water, with nothing to work with but a hunting knife, is a long and messy business. The real backbreaker is getting the meat back to camp. Even when quartered, the pieces weigh 150 to 250 pounds—more than most men want to attempt to handle. Pack horses, jeeps, and canoes all help to solve this problem.

A Yukon Territory guide told me that the Indians of the territory have a very practical solution. When they kill a moose, they just move their home, or camp, to where the moose fell and stay there until they have eaten all of it.

I have eaten moose meat only a few times and found it good although somewhat dry. It is best before the rutting season, for then the animals are in peak condition. Presumably cow meat (cows are also hunted in some areas) retains its flavor most of the year, but as the rutting season progresses, the meat of the bull becomes strong and unpalatable. After the rutting season the meat loses its offensive odor, but the bulls are in such poor condition that the meat is dry, tough, and tasteless.

Winter is never a pleasant time for wild creatures that must face the subzero temperatures of the north.

Winter

IN MOOSE COUNTRY winter comes early and stays late. It brings bitter cold and deep snows. It is a stern test for these animals, and only the hardy survive.

The first winter storms find bulls weak from their recent rutting. If the weather is not too severe in late autumn and early winter, they have time to rebuild their physical condition. But if heavy snows come early, many face a precarious and possibly fatal winter. Mature bulls generally shed their antlers by January 1. This may have some survival value, as during the worst winter weather they will not have to expend energy carrying these heavy headpieces around.

Yearlings that had been guided and protected through their first winter by solicitous mothers must now look after themselves.

Cows have the greatest responsibility through the winter. The safety and well-being of at least three animals may depend on a single cow. She must take care of herself first, as well as her six-month-old calf, which, although as large as an adult white-tailed deer, is dependent upon her to see it safely through its first tough winter season. An orphaned moose rarely survives the winter. Unrelated cows show little or no inclination to sponsor or protect a motherless calf. A pregnant cow also carries next spring's calf whose health at birth is largely determined by the mother's winter feed.

On December 17, 1969, I drove from Jackson, Wyoming, to the

A cow and her six-month-old calf feed on willow twigs.

entrance of the Colter Bay campground on Jackson Lake, a distance of about 43 miles; spent most of the day along the highway between Moran and the outlet to Jackson Lake; and returned to Jackson about sundown that evening. During that time I saw forty-seven moose. Twelve of them were feeding on the sagebrush flats in the area north of Moose Junction between the highway and the Snake River. There were two groups of four that appeared to be composed of young animals—yearlings, I judged. The groups were about a half-mile apart. Then there were two cow-calf groups at least a mile or more from any other visible animal. There was probably no more than 6 inches of snow on the level at the time. Since this was not enough to drive them from the willow bottoms along the Snake River, they may have been feeding in the sagebrush from choice.

It was still quite early in the morning when I turned west at Moran Junction and had to stop the car while a cow moose, with an amorous bull close behind her, trotted across the road in front of me. A few seconds later the cow's twin calves followed.

Several miles from Jackson Lake I met a group of five moose, composed of three bulls with apparently varying degrees of rutting drive still present and a cow and calf. In the big willow flats on the east side of Jackson Lake, I counted four bulls, two of which were

116

Mother and youngster resting in a foot of snow.

mature animals with large antlers. Near the Colter Bay campground entrance two bulls that looked to be two or three years old were out in a meadow nosing through a foot of snow for food. With them was what appeared, through the binoculars, to be a yearling cow. Not far from this group, two calves that were probably twins walked slowly across a broad snow-covered meadow. I spent a half-hour looking around for the cow, but the twins were either orphans or their mother was well hidden. All the other moose I saw were cows alone or cows with calves.

Two months previously I had photographed rutting groups in the willow flats east of Jackson Lake. There were more moose there during December than there had been in October. I had seen no moose during the October visit along the Snake River between Jackson Lake Dam and Moran Junction. Apparently the snow, although not yet of a depth to hamper moose travel, had prompted a gradual movement toward their wintering grounds 5 or so miles away, which in this area are the willow-covered creek bottoms where the snow depth seldom exceeds 2 or 3 feet. This amount of snow poses no threat to the animals unless it becomes heavily crusted. Then it is a hazard, and the sharp, icy crust may cut through the skin of their legs if they have to travel.

The moose's ability to move through snow depends to a great ex-

117

tent on its depth, density, and hardness. In chest-high snow, a moose must either bound or plow, both of which actions may lose the animal more than it gains, as the energy output necessary to reach a food source may be more than that supplied by the food consumed.

Moose seem to have little if any fear of ice covering lakes and streams. As soon as a strong coating covers the surface within their range, they put it to use. In Michigan the animals use the comparatively easy going of the ice to move along shorelines, feeding on evergreen forage. In British Columbia, moose tracks were found on ice where they had been breaking into muskrat houses, apparently to get something the muskrats had stored there to eat. It is presumed that the moose of Michigan's Isle Royale have crossed over from Canada on the frozen waters of Lake Superior, a distance of 15 miles. However, they sometimes misjudge the strength of the ice, break through, and drown.

Only deep, heavily crusted snow hampers a moose's movements.

Winter

When the snow gets deeper—30 inches or more—moose tend to restrict their movements, and several animals may be found in the same relatively small area if a good supply of food is present. Up to fifteen or twenty animals have been reported in such congregations, but this is unusual. Smaller groups and solitary animals are more common.

The presence of several animals moving from one feeding point to another in deep snow causes well-defined trails to be cut through the snow and creates what is known as a "moose yard." This is similar to the "yards" created by white-tailed deer, but moose do not use them so extensively, probably because it takes a lot more snow to immobilize the long-legged moose. If the animals remain concentrated long enough, the trails may become joined until most of the snow in that area is flattened. Additional snowfalls build up layers of packed snow and elevate the moose so they can reach browse at higher and higher levels.

During most of the winter, when the lakes and streams are frozen over, moose apparently satisfy their need for water by eating snow.

At times moose are forced to "yard up," as when there is a deep, crusted snow, but most often yarding is simply a natural gathering of moose on a favorable feeding ground. It is a temporary situation arising from the benefits of the food there rather than from the desire to be social. As soon as the forage becomes scarce, the group begins to disperse. Moose of eastern North America show more of a tendency to yard than do those in the West.

As long as the food holds out and they are not molested, moose do not move far during the winter. Some stay in the same area all year. Along some of the river bottoms, the Snake River especially, where there is an abundance of willow, there always seem to be moose regardless of the season.

Moose paw through the snow to get at low-lying plants, which they apparently locate by their sense of smell. However, there is a limit to

This bull moose is pawing through the snow to reach food.

the amount of snow through which they will dig, or possibly the limit is the amount of snow through which they can detect food.

When food is scarce they are able to break saplings as big as 2½ inches in diameter at the break to get at the tops. They have several ways of doing this. They can straddle a small sapling and "ride" it down. Or they reach high and push the trunk down with the muzzle and then slide the muzzle toward the tip until the tree breaks. Or, instead of pushing saplings down with the muzzle, moose may grasp them in the mouth and pull them down or bend them until they break. During extremely cold weather, trees are quite brittle and break much more easily than they do at higher temperatures, when the wood is more flexible. On clear, quiet days, the noise of the breaking is audible a long way off.

A cow moose feeding on aspen twigs.

The most important foods during the critical winter period in representative locations are:

Alaska: Willow, kenai birch, dwarf birch, aspen, alder.

British Columbia: Willow, aspen, service berry, maple, paper birch, red osier dogwood, false box.

Eastern North America: Balsam fir, hemlock, white cedar, willow, quaking aspen, balsam poplar, sweet gale, beaked hazelnut, yellow birch, gray birch, white birch, dwarf birch, alder, mountain ash, juneberry, striped (moose) maple, mountain maple, sugar maple, red maple, red osier dogwood, hobble bush, high bush cranberry, withe rod, sweet viburnum, red-berried elder.

Montana-Wyoming: Willow, alpine fir, aspen, service berry, chokecherry, lodgepole pine, cottonwood, red osier dogwood, silver berry.

As winter progresses and food supplies become critical, moose eat food that does little more than fill their stomachs without providing any real nutritional value. The young terminal tips, bud ends, and leaves, when they are present, contain most of the nutrients. But when shortages exist, moose consume much of the old two-year growth. Occasionally, they will even resort to feeding on some three-year-old wood. Since there is little food value in this material, the survival chances of the animals may be lowered.

Winter food shortages, either qualitatively or quantitatively, or both, produce malnutrition in moose, the effects of which can be quite serious and may cause losses in the population. These losses are not directly caused by the malnutrition but are a result of diseases or parasites that attack undernourished moose. If an animal is in very weakened condition, death may result.

Pregnant cows can, when winter food supplies are below minimum requirements, become so weakened that their calves may not come to term or, if they do, may be stillborn or born as weaklings unable to survive.

One of the most common diseases of moose is called "moose sickness" —probably because the manifestations of the sickness are so obvious and unusual. An afflicted animal is in a weakened and emaciated condition, loses its fear of man, and wanders aimlessly in circles. Or it may stay in one place and refuse to leave. Vision is affected and the animal becomes partly or totally blind. One or both ears may droop and the head hangs to the right or left. Partial paralysis of the legs follows until finally the animal is unable to rise or stand and it dies.

Some recent research indicates that moose sickness is caused by a small parasitic roundworm within the moose's nervous system. It migrates to the brain via the blood vessels and spinal cord. Moose sickness symptoms have not been found in animals over three and a half years old, which indicates that older animals develop an immunity or resistance to the parasite.

Other internal parasites that affect moose include liver flukes, tapeworms, other roundworms, stomach flukes, and lungworms.

Flies and mosquitoes represent no health hazard to moose, but during the summer they can be annoying. Some observers report that moose submerge themselves in water to avoid these flying pests. Most of the moose seen in water, however, are there to feed. Captive moose that took advantage of an old millpond to get away from insects spent hours lying in the water and mud with only parts of their heads exposed. They left the pond with a coating of mud which gave them some protection.

I watched a bedded calf one hot September day when the air was still and the flies were bad. I was constantly brushing at thousands of these insects, which seemed intent on getting into my eyes, my ears, and my nose. It was too far for me to actually see flies on the calf, but the constant motion of its ears indicated that there were as many around it as me. I was going to count the number of times the calf twitched its ears each minute but soon gave up because one or both were in constant motion. Other than that, the calf seemed un-

Scratching an itch.

affected by the swarms of insects.

The winter, or moose, tick is the only external parasite that is a serious health hazard to moose. This pest is most prevalent during late winter and spring. It seems to cause moose considerable irritation, which they alleviate by scratching with their hind feet or by rubbing against shrubs and trees. In the later stages of their development they use their antlers to scratch the hind legs. Tick infestations are extremely heavy at times, with thousands attached to a single animal. As many as 500 ticks have been found on each ear of a moose. Such attacks can be weakening though not fatal. Coupled with malnutrition or some disease, they can cause death.

Other diseases reported in moose include blindness, Bang's disease, tuberculosis, respiratory ailments, arthritis, and necrotic stomatitis. This last-named infection, which apparently accounted for many moose deaths on Isle Royale, occurs when a moose injures the tissues of its mouth by browsing on coarse twigs and the wound becomes infected. Death generally follows.

The seriousness of the effect of parasites and disease on moose populations varies in different localities. But even in those areas where

Crossing a highway can be dangerous for moose—and cars.

it does not appear to be a threat to populations, the cumulative effect of diseases through adults lost, cows that fail to conceive, cows that abort, calves that do not come to term, or weak calves that fail to survive can combine to produce a damaging blow to moose populations.

Some of the accidents that kill moose—drowning, for example—have already been discussed, but there are others that claim a fair number of animals in certain parts of the range. Some fall off cliffs, possibly while being chased. A few fall into construction ditches, trip over fallen trees, or become entangled in fences. Highway accidents kill quite a few, especially in winter when moose refuse to leave the easy travel route they find on a plowed highway. Forest fires undoubtedly kill moose.

Alaskan railroads have problems each winter because moose prefer to move along the plowed railroad right of ways rather than flounder through deep snowdrifts. Railroad crews try all sorts of stratagems to scare animals from the track—whistles, lights, flares, and so forth. Sometimes it works, but often it does not. Occasionally, an unusually aggressive big bull attacks the engine, usually with fatal results to

125

himself. In the spring of 1966, on a 40-mile stretch of the Alaska Railroad between Willow and Talkneeta, thirty-nine moose carcasses were counted. During winters with exceptionally deep snow, as many as two hundred moose have been killed on substantially this same stretch of railroad.

On a 127-mile stretch of railroad in Ontario, twelve moose were killed in one week in June 1948. Many of these train-caused deaths seem to result when the animals become confused by the glare of the headlights of an oncoming train.

The moose is not always the only loser in these encounters. Train derailments resulting from train-moose collisions have destroyed valuable equipment and cost the railroads many thousands of dollars.

Under severe winter conditions moose have been known to move into the protection of civilization and adopt yards, gardens, and similar sheltered areas. They have been seen wandering around city streets and often become such nuisances that they have to be destroyed.

A Montana resident who lives in moose country told me of a cow and a calf that moved into his barn one snowy night and spent the rest of the winter there. They caused no trouble other than that the overprotective cow chased every one away. Fortunately the barn had several entrances which permitted the rancher to reach the hay reserves he needed for his cattle and horses. Eventually a sort of armed truce evolved since there seemed no way of removing the moose other than killing them. They departed in the spring.

Moose manifest the tremendous will to survive that most wild animals seem to possess. I have seen three-legged deer and elk, and one-winged, flightless geese, that have made it even under severe winter conditions. In the February 1953 issue of *Wyoming Wildlife* magazine, T. W. "Bill" Daniels described a cow moose he saw that had been shot through the rear part of the lungs. She had a calf with her, and the two of them remained in a small area where they could forage on willow and aspen without much expenditure of effort. When the cow lay down in the snow she left blood stains from both sides of the wound and from her nose and mouth. Obviously she had been grievously hurt. Within two weeks the bleeding had stopped, and the cow, though still weak, moved about with greater ease as she browsed. Mr. Daniels believed that both cow and calf survived the winter.

Mr. Daniels spent some ten years at a feeding station in Wyoming where hay was supplied to elk during the winter. A few moose also took advantage of these handouts, and he described seeing a large bull moose completely dominated by a cow elk, and stated that even an elk calf will run a moose away from a pile of hay. However, bison when present dominate both moose and elk. Moose were more compatible with the horses at the feeding station than the elk—so much so, in fact, that they wanted to share the barn with the horses. They became so accustomed to man's presence that they would stand around with the horses, and even a slap on the rump would not move them.

Moose must feel more of a kinship with horses than they do with cows. Often they will mix with a herd of horses during a night's grazing but will rarely associate closely with cattle except during a bad winter when they help themselves to hay put out for the cattle.

Moose are so big and strong that predators are not much of a threat to them. The smaller ones—bobcat (*Lynx rufus*), lynx (*Lynx canadensis*), and coyote (*Canis latrans*)—are of no concern although they are all capable of killing a very young calf. The extremely effective protection provided by cows makes preying on moose calves a more hazardous undertaking than these three predators generally want to face. In very few months a moose calf is large enough—150 to 200 pounds—to give a good account of itself against these much smaller animals.

Wolverines (*Gulo luscus*) are reported to kill a moose calf once in a while, but the rarity of such reports indicates that these incidents are uncommon.

Cougars (*Felis concolor*) are apparently capable of killing moose

Bobcats (top), Canadian lynx (left), and coyotes (bottom) do not constitute much danger to healthy adult moose.

but do so rarely. I have found no authenticated record of a cougar killing a moose, but Cahalane (1947) reported that, in the northern Rockies, the cougar occasionally "makes a meal of a moose."

Black bears (*Ursus americanus*) are probably little, if any, threat to adult moose and would no doubt need to find one under exceptional circumstances in order to catch and kill it. Accounts of struggles between black bears and bull moose have been described in which the bears were killed or forced to climb trees for safety.

From his study of the behavior of moose in British Columbia, Valerius Geist reported observations of a large bull moose and a black bear 20 yards apart in a small meadow. The bull was lying down and the bear was feeding on vegetation. The bull looked

Black bears (right) are a threat to moose calves; mature moose can hold their own against them. Moose treat grizzlies (left) with a great deal of respect.

toward the bear for a while and then got up, moved a short distance away and started feeding. The bear paid no attention to the moose. Later the bull returned to its bed and lay down while the bear fed 10 yards away. On several other occasions moose moved off when black bears approached.

Alaskan moose in close association with black bears showed a somewhat similar reaction—a sort of watchful disregard, as if they considered black bears only a minor threat.

They are, however, suspected of many moose calf deaths in country where black bears are plentiful.* But the evidence of bear tracks

* *Editor's Note:* Mr. Van Wormer has thoroughly discussed the black bear's food habits in *The World of the Black Bear,* another Living World book.

around moose carcasses or moose hair in bear droppings are not con-
clusive proof that a bear made the kill, since bears readily eat carrion.

Moose treat the grizzly bear and the big brown bear,* largest
carnivore in North America, with a great deal more respect than they
do the black bear—which indicates the grizzly and the brown bear are
considered a greater threat. Grizzlies have killed adult moose in
Wyoming when spring snows caused the moose to flounder. In Jasper
National Park, Alberta, Canada, grizzlies feed extensively on elk and
moose, which they apparently run down and kill. Most of the grizzly
predation on moose in Yellowstone National Park takes place during
March, April, and May. Some has also been reported during the summer, but apparently by fall the weak moose have been weeded out
and the calves have grown enough to outrun a grizzly.

Alaskan moose have demonstrated their ability to outswim a mature
brown bear, and in a race between a moose cow accompanied by a
two- or three-week-old calf and a brown bear with two cubs, the
moose won. Nevertheless, the brown bear does kill some, but indi-
cations are that by the time the calves are three weeks or a month
old they have a good chance of escaping from the bear.

Wolves (*Canis lupus*), the major moose predators, do most of their
killing during the winter. In the summer, beaver, rabbits, and other
small game comprise a substantial part of a wolf's diet. The moose
that they do get during this season are generally calves. Moose are
always tough opponents and can kill or cripple a wolf with one blow
of a slashing front hoof or the smashing kick of a hind foot. In the
summer they take to the water and escape attack by wading out so

* *Editor's Note:* Robert L. Rausch (1963), after careful taxonomic studies of the grizzly
and brown bear, concluded that these are two races, or subspecies, of the same genus;
they are closely related to each other and at times cannot be told apart when seen in the
wild. They are *Ursus arctos horribilis*, the grizzly bear, silverback, roachback, or simply,
grizzly, and *Ursus arctos middendorffi*, often called big brown bear, Alaskan brown bear,
and Kodiak bear. See p. 180 of *The World of the Grizzly Bear* by W. J. Schoonmaker, a
Living World book.

The wolf is the major moose predator. This is the all-white (not albino) color phase found in the northern parts of the wolf's range.

deep that a wolf would have to swim to reach them—a situation that would be disastrous to the wolf.

But when the lakes freeze and the snow drifts deep, small game disappears or becomes scarce and wolves turn their attention almost entirely to moose. A lone wolf can kill a moose, but only if the animal is weakened by disease, crippling, or some other reason, or if it makes a mistake and puts itself at a disadvantage.

The World of the Moose

Isle Royale National Park, a 210-square-mile island in Lake Superior, has, in recent years, become an almost ideal laboratory for the study of the prey-predator relationship between wolf and moose.

For at least twenty years prior to 1950, the island had been ravaged by periodic population explosions of moose followed by periods of starvation and death. Sometime during the late 1940's wolves appeared on the island, probably reaching it by crossing from Canada on the frozen surface of Lake Superior. With an excessively high moose population to feed upon, the wolves lived well and no doubt produced maximum litters. It wasn't many years before the wolves were numerous enough to offset the overproduction of moose, and the populations of these species now exist in a more or less "balanced" state on the island, which has no other large predators and no other ungulates.

During the winter wolves travel in packs of varying numbers. One of the Isle Royale packs contains fifteen to sixteen animals; another, five to six. Packs of up to thirty have been reported in other areas. The larger of the Isle Royale packs averaged a moose kill every three or four days. The smaller pack made a kill about every tenth day. Each wolf eats an average of 13 pounds of flesh, hair, and bone each day. They do not, by any manner of means, kill every moose they start after. A dozen moose may be "tested" before a kill is made.*

Wolves approach a moose displaying their mounting excitement with wagging tails. Sometimes the moose will detect the wolves about the same time that the wolves detect it. At other times the pack approaches quite closely before the moose knows it is near. The moose may stand and defy its attackers. In this case the pack rings the quarry and makes repeated feints, as if to attack, but displays a great deal of

---

* *Editor's Note:* In *The World of the Wolf,* a Living World book, authors Russell J. Rutter and Douglas H. Pimlott document with drawings and text the route of four chases of deer by wolves to their conclusion, and show that not all hunts by wolves are successful.

respect for the moose's lethal feet. The moose retaliates with short charges and tries to trample its attackers or lashes out with its hoofs. If it stands its ground for a few minutes, the pack gets discouraged and leaves.

When the moose decides to run, the wolves take after it immediately and catch up rather quickly unless the moose has too much of a head start. However, sound, healthy ones can often outrun the pack. Wolves have difficulty in rough, thick growth and may give up the hunt when a moose takes them into such an area.

In snow up to 2 feet deep, wolves have the advantage. Over that depth, the long legs of moose prove their worth—unless the snow is crusted enough to support a wolf but not enough to support the much heavier moose. Then the fleeing animal is in real trouble. And it is usually a fatal mistake for a moose to try to travel over slippery ice to escape a pack.

While in pursuit, wolves seem to look for weaknesses. Once a moose displays any, they take advantage of it. Some animals are chased for a long way without being attacked, whereas others are set upon immediately. Probably, the timing is determined by the weakness seen. Attacks are made at the rump and flanks first. Several wolves sink their teeth into these parts and hang on, slowing the animal down. A single wolf may fasten its teeth in the moose's tender nose and cause the frantic animal to concentrate all its efforts on this one attacker. Moose have been seen to lift a wolf clear off the ground and swing it from side to side until finally it drops off. While this is happening, the rest of the pack is tearing away at the moose's hindquarters and legs, even jumping on top of its rump. Sorely hurt, the moose will stop and face its tormentors. But they back off and wait patiently. Even a badly injured moose is still a dangerous fighter.

If the moose tries to lie down to rest, the wolves start their harassment again, giving the animal no chance to recuperate. It may run again and suffer additional attacks. Eventually it becomes too ex-

133

hausted to run or fight back, and the wolves close in. In a few minutes the moose is dead.

A cow protects her calf from marauding wolves by following along behind the fleeing youngster, placing herself between it and the wolf pack. She may stop to slow the pursuers. Their aim is to separate the calf from the cow. If they can get it 25 yards from its mother, it does not have much of a chance. However, they are obviously not always successful.

Isle Royale moose studies disclosed the fact that most winter kills of moose are of animals less than one year old. The majority of the adults killed were estimated to be nine or ten years old and past their physical peak. The one- to six-year-old group seemed able to cope successfully with wolf attacks. Almost half of the animals killed by wolves during one study period had one or more disabilities—an indication that the aged and infirm are the principal targets of these predators.

A moose is considered in its prime between six and ten years of age, and its maximum age is eighteen to twenty-two years (Palmer, 1954). However, the average moose probably lives a much shorter life.

Moose captured as calves tame easily, and there are records of individuals trained to work under harness and to pull sleighs. Generally the animals become difficult to handle as they reach maturity, especially the bulls.

Attempts to keep moose in zoological gardens have not been entirely successful. The animals usually develop some sort of gastric disorder and die. This is attributed to the difficulty of providing foods equivalent to what they eat in the wild. Some of these captive animals develop a craving for rather strange foods. One became a tobacco addict, whereas a young one went all out for chocolate bars. Oranges and bananas appealed strongly to other captive moose.

Moose and Man

IN PRIMITIVE TIMES the moose was the mainstay of the Indians of Canada and the northern United States in regions where it lived. It was primarily a fine food source, contributing as much as 500 pounds or more of prime meat when a large bull was killed. The muffle, or nose, was considered a great delicacy. The heavy hide furnished clothing, moccasin leather, and material for snowshoes. Little was wasted: The back sinew was used by the squaws as sewing thread; the coarse, bristly mane furnished the material for embroidery; the antlers and bones were made into tools; hoofs were converted into rattles for use in religious ceremonies.

The first civilized men to see the American moose were the French *voyageurs* of the sixteenth century, the original explorers of northern North America. However, these first explorers provided only sketchy descriptions of the animals they encountered, and it was not until after Champlain's explorations in 1603 that the moose or "orignac" was described and recognized as being similar to the European elk.

These early explorers were obviously quite impressed with this giant animal and the necessities of life produced from it. One of the more literate among them wrote in 1632:

Their hids are by the Salvages converted into very good lether, and dressed as white as milke. Of this lether, the Salvages, make the best shoes, and use to barter away the skinnes to other Salvages, that have none of the kinde of bests in the parts where they live.

It didn't take the white man long to discover the value of moose. With the aid of his firearms he quickly made moose meat and skins important articles of commerce. The exploitation of moose by both Indians and whites soon brought about a noticeable decrease in moose populations all across the settled parts of eastern Canada and the northeastern United States. By 1800 the future of the moose was uncertain in many parts of its range.

The westward movement of the white man had both a good and a bad effect on the moose. It was mostly bad in the beginning due to overhunting, and moose populations declined steadily. Later, fortunately, extensive cutting of timber along with accidental and natural (lightning-caused) forest fires provided food and additional range for moose. Mostly the animals have not, nor are they likely to, come back in places subject to the extreme pressures of modern civilization.

Records of moose left by the early explorers and the first pioneers who moved west indicate that moose were common all across the northern states, with the exception of areas west of the Continental Divide. West of the Rocky Mountains, the early-day status of moose is obscure.

It has apparently been within recorded historical time that moose moved southward into Wyoming and into east-central Idaho. None of the early explorers or trappers who operated in the Jackson Hole area of northwestern Wyoming between 1810 and 1845 reported moose there, although they left records of other wildlife. By the late 1860's and early 1870's a few moose were seen in the Yellowstone National Park area. Apparently there was a gradual movement of moose somewhat southward. In 1912 a total of 47 moose was counted in Jackson Hole. By 1950 there was an estimated 2,600 moose in Wyoming, some 600 of which were thought to be in or around Jackson Hole. The Big

Game Inventory for 1968, previously mentioned, shows an estimated winter moose population of 700 in Grand Teton National Park, which no doubt can be considered the same as Jackson Hole.

Because of its size, unusual build, and the massive antlers of the male, the moose inspired some strange ideas and beliefs. Much of this began in Europe, where the Old World form of the moose was known long before the North American variety was discovered.

Pliny the Elder, a naturalist of the first century A.D., stated that the

Antlers were once believed to contain curative powers.

moose had no joints in its hind legs and was forced to lean against a tree to sleep. The upper lip was thought to be so long that the animal could only graze while backing up.

The left hind foot of a European elk (moose) was believed to cure epilepsy if part of it was worn, ground up in wine and drunk, or burned and inhaled. Next best thing for epilepsy was antlers, if taken from a moose on the first of September. Younger antlers, presumably obtained during the early stages of growth, were considered good treatment for snake bites if sliced and steeped in herbs and spirits. Moose fat was made into an ointment and its heart into a cure for heart trouble. Dried moose nerves cured arthritis, rheumatism, and cramps when wrapped around the afflicted limbs, and would prevent a recurrence if worn continuously.

Hunters in Europe were supposed to have lured moose into range by using violinists to play for them. Apparently, this was reasonably successful unless a tone-deaf moose was encountered or the musician was a bad violinist. On one occasion an enraged Swedish moose attacked and killed both hunter and musician.

The Indians of northern North America were well aware of the value of the great moose and did not neglect it in their songs and legends. An early French explorer reported that the Indians considered the moose an animal of good omen and believed that those who dreamed of them often could expect a long life.

It is probable that in the United States only a small percentage of the people, except in Alaska, have ever seen a live moose. Yet most of them are familiar with the name of the animal and have at least some idea of what one looks like. Even the youngest Americans recognize a moose because the animal's unusual appearance has been caricatured in animated cartoons seen regularly on television.

The bigness of the moose has caused its adoption as a word meaning "very large." A great many big American football players, for example, have been called "Moose."

Moose and Man

Many place names incorporate the word "moose." For example, there is Moosehorn National Wildlife Refuge in Maine; Moosehead Lake, the largest lake in Maine; moosewood, or striped maple, a small tree native to eastern North America; the Moose post office in Grand Teton National Park; Moose Falls in Yellowstone National Park; and many others. Of special interest is Moose Factory, a Canadian village in Ontario founded in 1671 by two French-Canadian explorers as a trading post—and still operating as such.

An American fraternal organization, founded in 1888, with approximately 1,250,000 members today, is called the Loyal Order of Moose. Its headquarters is in Mooseheart, Illinois, and it publishes the *Moose Magazine*.

At one time there was even an American political party named after the moose. It was an offshoot of the Republican Party and was popularly called the "Bull Moose Party." This name was the result of a comment by former President Theodore Roosevelt, who joined its ranks and became its presidential candidate. He is reported to have said, apparently in reply to some question about his health and fitness for the office of President, that he felt "fit as a moose."

Somewhere back in the misty reaches of time, the first man ever to see a moose probably looked upon the animal as nothing more than a giant-sized pot roast just waiting for him to figure out a way to kill it. In the thousands of years since then, man's attitude has changed little until comparatively recently, when a more aesthetic appreciation of moose and other wild animals has developed. Now the moose is considered a desirable species not only for its food value but as hunters' trophies and as fascinating animals that should be preserved.

The value of simply *seeing* moose, such as having them for park visitors to observe, is being rated higher and higher as our wild environment faces more and more compression due to the needs of our rapidly expanding population.

The mere presence of man in moose country does not seem to disturb the animals to any great extent, but excessive hunting and destruction of habitat will effectively move them.

When man and moose more or less share the same habitat, some conflicts are inevitable. As mentioned earlier, moose readily adopt railroad lines and snowplowed highways for their own and will dispute the right of way with engines and automobiles. Ranchers often find themselves unwilling providers of moose food during the winter, when the animals come into the fields and take stacked hay, or feed in the corrals alongside the cattle.

In some places electric fences have been tried as a means of keeping moose away from stored hay—but with little success. However, wooden panels 8 feet high laid against a haystack have worked fairly well.

Records seem to indicate that moose are more easily provoked into attacks on man during the winter, although there is no indication that the animals seek out people for that purpose. Probably the rigors of winter living tend to make the animals quick-tempered.

In Anchorage, Alaska, the Moose Run Golf Course reported having problems with, naturally, moose. For some reason or other, the flag sticks at the various holes attracted them, and their sharp hoofs did considerable damage to the carefully cultivated greens.

In a few regions, moose-browsing on some forest species, notably white birch and balsam fir, has been so severe as to deplete these resources seriously. Such a condition is detrimental to the moose population as well, for the animals can literally eat themselves out of house and home. Generally, a liberalization of hunting regulations takes care of any excessive moose population.

Where their ranges overlap, there is competition between white-tailed deer and moose for food during the winter, although there is no physical conflict between the species. Since the deer usually outnumber the moose, they can keep the browse clipped so close that it has little chance to grow enough to provide moose feed. Even though the moose can forage higher than the white-tailed deer, this advantage is short-lived if the young plants are overbrowsed and never grow up.

There are only a few places where elk and moose occur together, but even then there is little competition between them for food. The elk, primarily a grazer, eats some of the same browse eaten by moose but to such a limited extent that it is not a serious competitor.

The elk shares some of the moose's range, but there is little competition for food.

Mule deer, though browsers, do not seem to compete with the moose for winter forage, possibly because the deer tend to migrate to a different type of range.

Moose favor aquatic plants, often found in the waters above beaver dams.

Beaver have both good and bad effects on moose range. Beaver eat aspen and willow—both good moose foods—however, their dams maintain water levels or create shallow ponds and swampy areas which produce aquatic plants that are highly desirable moose food. But beaver-caused flooding may destroy some lowland willow browse.

Rabbits eat birch and willow shoots, which would grow into moose food, but they also eat spruce seedlings which tend to squeeze out the birch and willow. Mice help the moose by eating seeds of plants that choke out good moose foods.

This snowshoe rabbit is starting to change to its all-white winter coat.

Moose and Man

As the knowledge of game management increases, its complexities become more and more apparent. The answers are never simple, as management tries to achieve some sort of economic and ecologic balance between the plant and animal life in a given ecological system. It is known, for example, that timber-cutting leads to forest regeneration and the creation of several years of excellent moose forage where little if any existed before. However, it is not desirable to cut or destroy timber simply to create additional moose range.

The food problem with moose is much the same as that for other northern big game animals: winter forage, or rather the lack of it, which controls the number of animals a given area will support.

The amount of forage determines the number of moose on a given range.

Our efforts to protect our wildlife safeguard the future of the moose.

The ideal status, of course, is to achieve a population density of the maximum number of animals that can be maintained on the range without adversely affecting the quality of the range. Once this population level has been reached, it can be maintained only by removing a number of animals equal to the annual increase. To some extent this occurs naturally when overcrowding disperses some animals into new areas. This in itself is not always desirable, since there is the possibility of another animal species being involved whose territory and food supply may be threatened.

Oddly enough, either too many or too few moose on a range cause it to become less favorable for moose. If overpopulation exists, regrowth of shrubs and trees is adversely affected. If there are too few moose, the forest growth matures beyond the stage where it is favorable for moose.

The population density of a given area is not necessarily an indication of maximum usage of the range. A poor range can accommodate only a small number of moose, whereas ranges with good forage support many more animals in a comparable space.

There are and will continue to be encroachments upon the moose's range by so-called progressive projects. But the growing awareness on the part of the general public of the need to protect our environment and its wildlife, and the knowledge we have of how to manage wildlife populations, leads me to be optimistic about the future of the moose.

Moose Classification

THERE ARE SEVEN living subspecies of moose in the world, one in Europe, the European elk, *Alces alces alces* (Linnaeus); two in Asia, the Manchurian elk, *Alces alces cameloides* (Milne-Edwards), and the Siberian elk, *Alces alces pfizenmayeri* (Zukowsky); and four in North America.

The names and ranges of the North American subspecies are from *List of North American Recent Mammals* by Gerrit S. Miller, Jr., and Remington Kellogg (1955). I have added some common names.

Alces alces americana (Clinton): Eastern moose. Range: Wooded parts of eastern Canada, except Prince Edward Island, from Nova Scotia and New Brunswick westward through Quebec to eastern Ontario; southward formerly through Maine, Vermont, New Hampshire, northwestern Massachusetts, and New York.

Alces alces andersoni (Peterson): Northwestern moose. Range: Northern Michigan and Minnesota, western Ontario, westward to central British Columbia, north to eastern Yukon Territory and Mackenzie delta, Northwest Territories; southward formerly to Red River Valley and Turtle Mountains region of North Dakota and northern Wisconsin.

149

Alces alces shirasi (Nelson): Yellowstone or Wyoming moose. Range: Western Wyoming, eastern and northern Idaho, and western Montana, northward into southeastern British Columbia. Formerly in Blue Mountains of southeastern Washington and recorded also in Ferry County, northeastern Washington. Accidental in northeastern Utah.

Alces alces gigas (Miller): Alaskan moose. Range: Wooded parts of Alaska, western Yukon in Northwest Territories, and northwestern British Columbia.

The most practical way to determine to which subspecies a moose belongs is by the region in which it is found. This is especially true of the Yellowstone, Eastern, and Northwestern moose, all of which are medium-sized animals. The Yellowstone moose is somewhat lighter colored, but this is probably noticeable only when another subspecies is nearby for comparison. The Alaskan moose, of course, is much larger, but it, too, is most easily identified by the place in which it lives.

Bibliography

Allen, Durward L., and L. David Mech, "Wolves Versus Moose on Isle Royale," *National Geographic* (1963), 123:200–219.

Altmann, Margaret, "Patterns of Social Behavior in Big Game," *Transactions of Twenty-First North American Wildlife Conference* (1956). Washington, D.C.: Wildlife Management Institute. Pp. 538–545.

————, "Life with Mother," *Animal Kingdom* (1957), 60:79–80.

————, "The Social Integration of the Moose Calf," *Animal Behavior* (1958), 6:155–159.

————, "Group Dynamics in Wyoming Moose During the Rutting Season," *Journal of Mammalogy* (1959), 40:420–424.

————, "The Role of Juvenile Elk and Moose in the Social Dynamics of Their Species," *Zoologica* (1960), 45:35–39.

————, " 'Teen-Age' Problems in the Wilderness," *Animal Kingdom* (1961), 64:41–44.

Bailey, Vernon, "Our North American Moose," *Nature Magazine* (1940), 33:269–272.

Bassett, Neil R. "Winter Browse Utilization and Activities of Moose on the Snake and Buffalo River Bottoms of Jackson Hole, Wyoming." M.S. Thesis, Utah State Agricultural College, Logan, Utah, 1951.

Benson, Denis Andrew, "Nova Scotia Moose Studies." M.S. Thesis. University of Maine, Orono, Maine, 1955.

Bierwirth, Robert, "The Raising and Feeding of Moose," *Parks and Recreation Magazine* (1954), 37:21–22.

Boone and Crockett Club. *Records of North American Big Game*. New York: Holt, Rinehart & Winston, 1964.

Bourlière, François. *The Natural History of Mammals*. New York: Alfred A. Knopf, Inc., 1964.

Breckenridge, W. J., "Weights of a Minnesota Moose," *Journal of Mammalogy* (1946), 27:90–91.

Brooks, James W., "A Record of North America's Most Westerly Moose," *Journal of Mammalogy* (1953), 34:396–397.

Brown, Robert C., and James R. Simon, "Notes on Wintering Moose," *Wyoming Wildlife* (1947), 11:4–8.

Burt, W. H., and R. P. Grossenheider. *A Field Guide to the Mammals*. Boston: Houghton Mifflin Company, 1952.

Cahalane, Victor H. *Mammals of North America*. New York: The Macmillan Company, 1947.

Cameron, Eric, "Moose Are Mighty Dangerous," *Field & Stream* (1953), 59:35–37, 117–121.

Caras, Roger A. *North American Mammals*. New York: Meredith Press, 1967.

Carrington, Richard. *The Mammals*. New York: Time Incorporated, 1963.

Chatelain, Edward F., "Bear-Moose Relationships on the Kenai Peninsula," *Transactions of the Fifteenth North American Wildlife Conference* (1950). Washington, D.C.: Wildlife Management Institute. Pp. 224-234.

Daniels, T. W. "Bill," "Winter at Blackrock," *Wyoming Wildlife* (1953), 17:20–27.

Denniston, Rollin H., "Ecology, Behavior and Population Dynamics of the Wyoming or Rocky Mountain Moose, *Alces alces shirasi*," *Zoologica* (1956), 41:105–118.

de Vos, A., "Summer Studies of Moose in Ontario," *Transactions of the Twenty-First North American Wildlife Conference* (1956). Washington, D.C.: Wildlife Management Institute. Pp. 510–525.

————, "Summer Observations of Moose Behavior in Ontario," *Journal of Mammalogy* (1958), 39:128–139.

Dodds, Donald Gilbert. "A Contribution to the Ecology of the Moose in Newfoundland." M.S. Thesis, Cornell University, Ithaca, New York, 1955.

———, "Observations of Pre-rutting Behavior in Newfoundland Moose," *Journal of Mammalogy* (1958), 39:412–416.

———, "Feeding and Growth of a Captive Moose Calf," *Journal of Wildlife Management* (1959), 23:231–232.

Dufresne, Frank, "Too Many Moose!" *Field & Stream* (1952), 57:54–57.

Edwards, R. Yorke, and Ralph W. Ritcey, "The Migrations of a Moose Herd," *Journal of Mammalogy* (1956), 37:486–494.

———, "Reproduction in a Moose Population," *Journal of Wildlife Management* (1958), 22:261–268.

Findley, James S., "A Record of Moose Speed," *Journal of Mammalogy* (1951), 32:116.

Geist, Valerius, "On the Behaviour of the North American Moose (*Alces alces andersoni* Peterson 1950) in British Columbia," *Behaviour* (1963), 20:377–416.

Gregory, Tappan. *Deer at Night in the North Woods.* Baltimore: Charles C. Thomas, 1930.

Hall, E. Raymond, and Keith R. Kelson. *The Mammals of North America.* New York: The Ronald Press Company, 1959.

Hamilton, W. J., Jr. *American Mammals.* New York: McGraw-Hill Book Company, 1939.

Harry, G. Bryan, "Winter Food Habits of Moose in Jackson Hole, Wyoming," *Journal of Wildlife Management* (1957), 21:53–57.

Hatter, James. "The Moose of Central British Columbia." Ph.D. Thesis, The State College of Washington, Pullman, Washington, 1950.

Hickie, Paul F. *Michigan Moose.* Game Division, Michigan Department of Conservation (no date).

Hoover, Helen, "The Moose," *Audubon Magazine* (1958), 60:210–213.

Hosley, N. W. *The Moose and Its Ecology.* Fish and Wildlife Service Leaflet 312, U.S. Department of Interior (1949).

Houston, Douglas B. *The Shiras Moose in Jackson Hole, Wyoming.* Technical Bulletin No. 1, Grand Teton Natural History Association (1968).

Kellum, Ford, "Cusino's Captive Moose," *Michigan Conservationist* (1941), 10:4–5.

Kelsall, John P., "Structural Adaptations of Moose and Deer for Snow," *Journal of Mammalogy* (1969), 50:302–310.

Knowlton, Frederick F., "Food Habits, Movements and Populations of Moose in the Gravelly Mountains, Montana," *Journal of Wildlife Management* (1960), 24:162–170.

LeResche, Robert E., "Behavior and Calf Survival in Alaskan Moose." M.S. Thesis, University of Alaska, Anchorage, Alaska, 1966.

McMillan, John F., "Some Feeding Habits of Moose in Yellowstone Park," *Ecology* (1953), 34:102–110.

————, "Some Observations on Moose in Yellowstone Park," *American Midland Naturalist* (1954), 52:392–399.

Mech, L. David, "Timber Wolf and Moose of Isle Royale," *Naturalist* (1963), 14:12–15.

————. *The Wolves of Isle Royale*. Fauna Series No. 7, Department of the Interior (1966).

Merrill, Samuel. *The Moose Book*. New York: E. P. Dutton & Company, 1916.

Moisan, Gaston, "Late Breeding in Moose, *Alces alces*," *Journal of Mammalogy* (1956), 37:300.

Moyle, John B., editor. *Big Game in Minnesota*. Technical Bulletin No. 9, Minnesota Department of Conservation (1965).

Murie, Adolph, "The Moose of Isle Royale." Misc. Publications, Museum Zoology, University of Michigan, No. 25 (1934), pp. 1–44.

————. *A Naturalist in Alaska*. New York: The Devin-Adair Company, 1961.

Murie, Olaus. *A Field Guide to Animal Tracks*. Boston: Houghton Mifflin Company, 1954.

O'Conner, Jack, and George C. Goodwin. *The Big Game Animals of North America*. New York: Outdoor Life and E. P. Dutton & Co., Inc., 1961.

Palmer, L. J., "Food Requirements of Some Alaskan Game Mammals," *Journal of Mammalogy* (1944), 25:49–54.

Palmer, Ralph S. *The Mammal Guide*. Garden City: Doubleday & Company, Inc., 1954.

Bibliography

Peek, James M., "Studies of Moose in the Gravelly and Snowcrest Mountains, Montana," *Journal of Wildlife Management* (1962), 26:360–365.

Peterson, Randolph L. *North American Moose*. Toronto: University of Toronto Press, 1955.

———. *The Mammals of Eastern Canada*. Toronto: Oxford University Press, 1966.

Pimlott, Douglas H., "Reproduction and Productivity of Newfoundland Moose," *Journal of Wildlife Management* (1959), 23:381–401.

Rausch, Robert L. "Some Aspects of Population Dynamics of the Railbelt Moose Populations, Alaska." M.S. Thesis, University of Alaska, Anchorage, Alaska, 1959.

———, "Geographic Variations in Size in North American Brown Bears, *Ursus arctos* L., as Indicated by Condylobasal Length," *Canadian Journal of Zoology*, Vol. 41 (1963).

———. *Report on 1965–1966 Moose Studies*. Alaska Department of Fish and Game (1967). Mimeographed.

Ray, Grace E., "Wazee, Ranch Moose," *Nature Magazine* (1958), 41:191–192.

Ritcey, R. W., and R. Y. Edwards, "Parasites and Diseases of the Wells Gray Moose Herd," *Journal of Mammalogy* (1958), 39:139–145.

Rutter, Russell J., and Douglas H. Pimlott. *The World of the Wolf*. New York and Philadelphia: J. B. Lippincott Company, 1968.

Scott, William Berryman. *A History of Land Mammals in the Western Hemisphere*. New York: The Macmillan Company, 1937.

Seton, Ernest Thompson. *Life Histories of Northern Mammals*. New York: Charles Scribner's Sons, 1909.

Severinghaus, C. W., "Tooth Development and Wear as Criteria of Age in the White-tailed Deer," *Journal of Wildlife Management* (1949), 13:195–216.

Smith, C. F., "Speed of Some Wild Mammals," *Journal of Mammalogy* (1943), 24:262–265.

Spencer, David L., and Edward F. Chatelain, "Progress in the Management of the Moose of South Central Alaska," *Transactions of the Eighteenth North American Wildlife Conference* (1953). Washington, D.C.: Wildlife Management Institute. Pp. 539–552.

Stebbings, E. L., "The Mightiest Moose Killer," *Field & Stream* (1953), 58:41, 112–113.

Straley, James, *"Alces shirasi,* the Newcomer," *Wyoming Wildlife* (1969), 33:9–14.

Telfer, Edmund S., "Comparison of a Deer Yard and a Moose Yard in Nova Scotia," *Canadian Journal of Zoology* (1967), 45:485–490.

Thompson, W. K., "Observations of Moose Courting Behavior," *Journal of Wildlife Management* (1949), 13:313.

Wulf, Lee, "All This and a White Moose, Too," *Outdoor Life* (1962), 130:46–49, 92–96.

Index